TAROT FOR BEGINNERS

THE HANGED MAN.

THE FOOL.

THE MOON.

QUEEN of WANDS.

III

V

XV

THE DEVIL.

IX

THE HERMIT.

VI

VIII

III

ACE of WANDS.

II

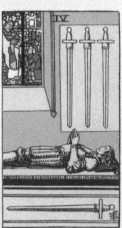

IV

II

VII

X

IV

XIII

TAROT
FOR BEGINNERS

A Holistic Guide to Using the Tarot
for Personal Growth & Self-Development

MEG HAYERTZ

ALTHEA
PRESS

Cover Photography © Lucia Lioso

Illustrations from the Rider-Waite Tarot Deck® reproduced by permission of U.S. Games Systems, Inc., Stamford, CT 06902 USA. Copyright © 1971 by U.S. Games Systems, Inc. Further reproduction prohibited. The Rider-Waite Tarot Deck® is a registered trademark of U.S. Games Systems, Inc.

ISBN: Print 978-1-62315-965-8 | eBook 978-1-62315-966-5

To my readers who believe
in the magic of art, which is to
say, the magic of reality—
and to those who wish to believe.

CONTENTS

Introduction viii

PART 1
GETTING STARTED

1 Tarot Then & Now 2

2 Tarot Mechanics 10

3 Common Card Spreads & Sample Readings 28

4 Growing from the Tarot 62

PART 2
THE CARDS

5 The Major Arcana 70

0. The Fool 72

I. The Magician 74

II. The High Priestess 76

III. The Empress 78

IV. The Emperor 80

V. The Hierophant 82

VI. The Lovers 84

VII. The Chariot 86

VIII. Strength 88

IX. The Hermit 90

X. Wheel of Fortune 92

XI. Justice 94

XII. The Hanged Man 96

XIII. Death 98

XIV. Temperance 100

XV. The Devil 102

XVI. The Tower 104

XVII. The Star 106

XVIII. The Moon 108

XIX. The Sun 110

XX. Judgement 112

XXI. The World 114

6 The Minor Arcana: Cups 116

7 The Minor Arcana: Pentacles 132

8 The Minor Arcana: Swords 148

9 The Minor Arcana: Wands 162

Conclusion 179   Appendix: Cards & Keywords Quick Reference 180

Resources 186   References 188   Index 189

INTRODUCTION

I RECEIVED MY FIRST TAROT READING at a psychic fair in Portland, Oregon. I knew nothing about psychics or the tarot. I was home from college for winter break, and my mom suggested we go to the fair. I was mostly there for the fanciful novelty I assumed intuitive and psychic arts to be, so I didn't have any expectations.

The tarot reader, however, immediately shed light on my challenges and joys. As she read my cards, she helped me name the pain I was experiencing in a long-distance relationship at that time, and she did something that nineteen-year-old me had never thought to do before: She placed my feelings of anger and longing within the context of the bigger timeline of my life. Feelings I had been drowning in now had finite shapes. I was allowed the fresh air of perspective and hope.

Following that reading, my mind opened in curiosity and my heart stopped silencing itself. Instead of continuing to waste much of my energy hating my life and blaming others for my unhappiness, I became more connected to the people in my life and more deeply fascinated by the mystery of my experience—as well as by the tarot cards, the tool that had helped me open to my own experience. I became more emotionally present in my life and in my writing.

A few years later, I began studying the tarot. I was so captivated by the cards that I found myself dedicating three months of intensive book study to learning the tarot. Through readings for friends and family, I soon discovered that I had been trained in intuition my entire life through the craft of writing. My BA with Honors in Creative Writing from Knox College and my MFA in Writing and Consciousness from California Institute of Integral Studies honed my skills of connecting the concrete details of an individual's life to abstract themes to create a powerful, poetic, and healing narrative.

My conviction in the fundamental connection of the intuitive crafts of writing and tarot reading was solidified during a workshop taught by one of my writing mentors, Regina Louise, in which Regina asked a couple of the writers in the group to offer a few details about important moments from their lives. From these details, Regina divined incredible personal mythologies for each person, weaving beauty from pain using a perfect, dynamic balance of the concrete and abstract—the same alchemical balancing act of reading tarot cards.

To get practice reading tarot cards, I offered free readings to everyone I knew. Most people took me up on my offer, then asked for another reading, and another. The depth we were able to achieve during these readings put me profoundly at ease. I loved holding space for my clients to sit with issues they did not otherwise know how to confront, as the tarot reader in Portland had done for me. Six months after I picked up my first book on the tarot, I had enough demand to start reading professionally.

I found, however, that many of my clients did not like hanging out in the abyss of the unknown as much as I did. Rather, they wanted me to tell them what to "do." But "doing" before reflecting, accepting, and *just being* in our inner experience rarely works.

When I read tarot for writers and artists, they knew exactly what to "do" with the themes and complexities we so tenderly uncovered during our sessions. They would become energized. The slouch they walked in with disappeared and the tiredness left their eyes. "I can't wait to go paint (or write, or sing) about this!" they'd call over their shoulder as they dashed out the door of my apartment. Through their craft, these artists had been trained to deal with the unknown, with the grandiose, and with pain. They were ready to express what they were experiencing, ready to let the resulting momentum and growth take over their life and lead them to new experiences, creative projects, and levels of meaning they'd never before imagined.

Tarot constantly supports me to access my intuition and put it into play in my daily life. When I was first building my business and could see no evidence of my success in the outside world, the tarot helped me recognize the inner and outer groundwork I was laying.

Because of the energy and clear purpose that my tarot readings gave my artist clients, I began reading cards exclusively for writers, artists, performers, and academics—as well as for anyone who aspired to unleash their creative voice, whether that is through art or any other form of self-expression, including business, social justice, and relationships.

I've come to believe that it is not enough to use the cards to merely shine a light on our inner world. If we want to grow, we have to pair insight with a skill set for integrating that insight into our conscious actions. Striving for creative expression and integrity in our personal lives and in our communities is how I suggest we use the 78 archetypes of the tarot to empower ourselves to become more loving and free.

It can be hard to connect big themes and spiritual ideas to the specific details of our daily lives, which often feel less than mythic. The tarot is a wonderful tool for cultivating this awareness, but not all beginner tarot books provide readers with techniques for actually relating the abstract archetypes and symbols in the cards to the specifics of their lives, nor for channeling the momentum of the resulting insights into their daily actions. It takes practice to develop these skills, and often people who are new to reading tarot don't know where to start. Even instructions such as "use your intuition" and "be creative" can be more daunting than helpful.

To that end, this book provides you with exercises and a clear method for practicing the skills of connecting your intuition and inner awareness with your mind and actions—connecting the themes of your life with your day-to-day experience—so that such a practice soon becomes second nature, and you find your life to be more inspiring, meaningful, and satisfying.

Through the more than one thousand readings I've done, I've seen the tarot help my clients find the clarity and courage to write and publish novels; land dream jobs; resolve conflicts; accept and love themselves; release the anxiety, shame, or resentment that had been holding them back; leave unhealthy marriages; cultivate more social justice in their communities; bring more love into broken relationships with their parents or children; meet life partners; and live more meaningful lives.

Personally, the tarot constantly supports me to access my intuition and put it into play in my daily life. When I was first building my business and could see no evidence of my success in the outside world, the tarot helped me recognize the inner and outer groundwork I was laying. The cards helped me trust my intuition to keep going despite the roadblocks. I was able to persevere, develop a practice that humbles and satisfies me, connect with a beautiful clientele, and write this book for you today.

The guidance I offer you in this book will help you connect with your intuition, heighten your awareness of the larger themes in your life, and grow into the satisfying, beautiful life you have been yearning for. Enjoy!

PART 1

GETTING STARTED

1

TAROT THEN & NOW

TAROT IS A SPIRITUAL TOOL that guides us to profound insight. The cards prompt our creativity and our connection to ourselves, others, the earth, and the divine. Tarot helps us experience the boundlessness of life. While the tarot shines a light on the spiritual experiences of limitlessness, the 78 cards themselves came about within our finite, limited world. The timeless archetypes were received, developed, shaped, analyzed, and depicted by people belonging to particular moments in history, which both limited and inspired them. In this chapter, we explore a brief history of the tarot. We'll look at possible origins of the playing cards, spiritual traditions associated with their imagery, and how these playing cards came to be used for divination.

ORIGINS

Table games and playing cards have been associated with divination off and on since their inception. We seem to have an instinct for playing with our fate in search of more satisfaction, meaning, or a thrill. When stakes are high in a game or in life, we can start to read into our situation, looking urgently for clues that will help us end the uncertainty and gain control of our fate. In this way, divination and gambling, while opposites in some ways, may have both arisen from the same impulse to master our fate.

A recurring message in this book is that the mundane and the spiritual have a complicated, yet fundamental relationship that can sometimes be slippery to pin down. The tarot is a tool we use to bridge these separate but interconnected spheres of our lives.

Where Did the Cards Come From?

The tarot deck is comprised of the Major Arcana (referred to as key or trump cards) and the Minor Arcana. The early Major Arcana cards were likely modeled after the floats called "triumphs" in an Italian pre-Lent festival parade predating Carnival and Mardi Gras; they featured a blend of Christian, Gnostic, and Pagan imagery. The Minor Arcana is very similar to our standard playing card deck, comprising ace through king of four suits (with the addition of one extra court card per suit).

What Is an Archetype?

Archetypes are characters, themes, and images that appear in myths, stories, and religions throughout the world, across time. Archetypal characters include the mother figure, the wise old man, and the joker—in the tarot deck, these are The Empress, The Hermit, and The Fool. Carl Jung , the founder of analytical psychology, put forth that all people relate to these archetypes and understand one another through them.

The standard playing cards we use for games like poker and go fish likely originated in the Persian Empire before the Islamic conquest of the seventh century. As Paul Huson describes in his book, *Mystical Origins of the Tarot*, these playing cards were brought to the Arab Mamluk Sultanate in Egypt in the thirteenth century, then, in the fourteenth century, to Europe.

In the fifteenth century, Filippo Maria Visconti, ruler of the Duchy of Milan, commissioned a deck of playing cards, likely as a gift to his daughter, Bianca Maria Visconti, upon her marriage to Francesco Sforza, future Duke of Milan. This deck, now known as the Visconti-Sforza Tarot, combined the standard playing card deck (as we know it) with an additional 22 cards, which became the Major Arcana. Though likely not the first deck of tarot, the Visconti-Sforza Tarot is the oldest known tarot deck.

The game tarot (beginning in Italy as *trionfi*, "triumphs") became a popular card game throughout Europe. It was a trick-taking card game in which each card was assigned a value, and players took turns drawing and discarding cards with the aim of winning with the highest value of cards.

How Did Tarot Become a Popular Form of Divination?

When Napoleon invaded Egypt at the turn of the eighteenth century, artifacts were stolen from Egypt and taken to Europe. This spawned a popular interest in Egypt among Europeans, and a curiosity about ancient traditions of mysticism and the occult became something of a fad in Europe. Around this time, people began using tarot cards for divination. Occult decks were produced specifically for the purpose of divination and demand grew high.

Many false histories of the tarot were created—and widely accepted as truth—in order to imagine its origins as ancient and mystic. In the mid-eighteenth century, Antoine Court de Gébelin, a Protestant pastor and Freemason, invented a widely accepted history that located the origin of the tarot in Ancient Egypt. He also suggested a link between the Kabbalah (the tradition of Jewish mysticism) and the tarot.

A French occultist, Éliphas Lévi, then created an extensive system linking elements of the Kabbalah with the Major and Minor Arcana. Lévi made a widely accepted claim that the tarot's origins were Kabbalistic.

In 1887, the Hermetic Order of the Golden Dawn, an organization dedicated to the study of the occult, was founded in England. One of its members, A. E. Waite, went on to compile occult symbolic systems and divination techniques, including astrology, that were or could become related to the tarot. He asked artist and fellow Golden Dawn member Pamela Colman Smith to illustrate a deck of tarot cards that utilized these symbols. Their deck was published by the London publisher William Rider & Son in 1910.

The Rider-Waite-Smith deck is still in print and enjoying continued popularity as a divinatory tool. It is considered to be the standard tarot deck. It has inspired hundreds, if not thousands, of tarot decks based on its 78 archetypes, ranging from the Collective Tarot and Hip Hop Tarot to Osho Zen Tarot and more.

PUTTING THE TAROT TO USE

Reading the tarot can do more than offer a window into one's potential future. It allows us to gain perspective on our current circumstances, make decisions, and develop self-knowledge, intuition, and creativity. Many influences—conscious and

The Woman Who Brought the Tarot to Life

THE HIGH PRIESTESS.

Pamela Colman Smith was the artistic designer of the Rider-Waite-Smith tarot deck. Using A. E. Waite's research and her own inspired intuition, she took artistic license with the cards, transforming the Minor Arcana with figures and landscapes and adding layers of imagery and atmosphere to the Major Arcana.

Colman Smith was born in London in 1878 to American parents and grew up traveling between cities and continents—from Manchester and London to Brooklyn and Jamaica. As an adult, she was very involved in international art, literature, theater, and politics. She designed sets and costumes with an international theater group and provided illustrations to authors such as W. B. Yeats and Bram Stoker (the author of *Dracula*), as well as for the women's suffrage movement. She hosted salons and published many books and a magazine series. She was synesthetic, meaning that some of her senses were neurologically linked to one another. Colman Smith could see sounds, and she painted images of music by Beethoven, Schumann, and Tchaikovsky.

In 1907, when she was 28, she was given a show by now-famous photographer and influential promoter of European and American modern art, Alfred Stieglitz, at his Little Galleries of the Photo-Secession in New York. His gallery had previously been devoted entirely to photography, but Colman Smith's paintings moved Stieglitz so much that he accepted her request for an exhibition. Her work received a rave review in the *New York Sun* that drew crowds and brought attention to Stieglitz as a curator. Though most of Colman Smith's paintings at the exhibition were sold and her reviewer lauded her skill above that of Edvard Munch, the show actually served as a turning point in Stieglitz's career, rather than Colman Smith's. ➡

As a woman, Colman Smith's artwork received little acknowledgment, much to her frustration and dismay. Even the name of the deck she designed is usually referred to as the Rider-Waite deck, omitting her name entirely. In recent years, there has been a push to represent her artistic interpretation and contribution to the tarot. Her and Waite's deck is now more frequently referred to as the Rider-Waite-Smith deck. Colman Smith herself, however, died penniless and in obscurity in 1951.

Pamela Colman Smith's artwork has made the tarot more evocative, accessible, meaningful, and profoundly spiritual for the millions of people who have found guidance within the images of the Rider-Waite-Smith deck. As James Gibbons Huneker, her *New York Sun* reviewer, wrote, "Pamela Colman Smith is a young woman with that quality rare in either sex—imagination."

unconscious, rational and irrational—converge in a tarot reading. For this reason, the tarot helps us align our various ways of knowing. Simultaneously, it helps us draw connections between areas of our life that would otherwise be separated by time, location, or modes of being. We don't have to leave our heart at home when we go to work, isolate our spirit to our place of worship, or keep our rational mind away from our emotions. The connections we draw when reading the tarot help us feel more whole and alive in all areas of our lives.

WHERE'S THE MAGIC?

Magic—also spelled *magick*, to differentiate it from the sensationalized performance of stage magicians—is the practice of working one's will according to unseen forces, usually to enact a vision that is collectively beneficial and which respects nature. Magic also encompasses divination, or the perception of those unseen forces and bigger vision, as in the tarot.

Though in common parlance, the word *magic* encompasses any inexplicable or supremely awe-inspiring occurrence, the English occultist of the early twentieth century, Aleister Crowley, emphasized that magick, specifically, was any action taken toward fulfilling one's larger purpose—including ordinary acts. I second Crowley's inclusion of the ordinary, or mundane, in the overall category of magic, as I find it ultimately difficult to differentiate observable facts and phenomena from the dazzling, mysterious essence that fills them.

Divination, regarded as a form of magic by believers and nonbelievers alike, to me describes any technique for gaining information about the unknown (including the future) using nonscientific methods. I consider making art to be a form of divination, as that process yields insight beyond the scope of rational thought, as well as most forms of meditation, since a meditation practice can bring self-knowledge and spiritual knowledge from beyond our rational mind. I hope to convey over the course of this book the falseness of the idea that there is a division between the magical, or divine, and the ordinary. That purported division has divided us from ourselves; however, the tarot helps us rebuild our wholeness.

False methods of divination have certainly been used throughout history to manipulate and make grabs at power and fame. Honest divination, however, is not trickery, but rather a practice of resisting the temptation to let our intellectual minds control our experience in order to honor the wisdom in our bodies, emotions, and the natural world.

Such knowledge isn't sentimental, whimsical, or optional. If we are to live in good conscience with ourselves, each other, and the earth that gives us life, then relational, intuitive forms of knowledge are absolutely necessary. The general disdain with which divination is sometimes regarded is, I believe, an oppressive attempt to delegitimize nonscientific ways of knowing and being by

"The suggestive imagery used in the trumps and court cards resonated with that part of people's psyches from which dreams and visionary experience spring. This mystical quality may have led naturally to the evolution of the cards as a divination tool . . ."
—PAUL HUSON, *Mystical Origins of the Tarot*

lumping them together and placing them in the same category as hoaxes and fanciful thinking.

While we must be rigorous, conscientious, and honest in our pursuit of meaning, we do not need to rely exclusively on logic. The effectiveness of the tarot as a divinatory tool comes from a combination of ways of knowing. These include spiritual traditions that have become intricately associated with the cards, as well as the universal and culturally based archetypes and symbols featured in the cards, which resonate in our subconscious, unlocking knowledge. Ultimately, the layers of our experience are endlessly rich and nuanced. Meaning exists within everything, waiting to spill forth at the smallest prompt.

Spiritual Traditions

As mentioned earlier, the Major Arcana reflects Gnostic, Catholic, and Pagan imagery, but there are also many spiritual traditions that have come to be associated with the cards, such as astrology,

Best Practices for Beginners

THE SUN.

JUDGEMENT.

One of the ways in which the tarot helps us refine our intuition—our ability to know or understand without conscious reasoning—is by reflecting a hunch or a barely conscious thought we've had prior to pulling a card. Among other things, the cards often offer confirmation of our premonitions about the larger significance of our present situation. (For example, we may be in a time in our life when we know we're supposed to be worried, but inexplicably, we aren't. We pull a card and see that we are awakening to a higher calling, as in Judgement, or that things are about to clear up, as in The Sun.) The more often we use the cards and receive their external confirmation, which helps us become more conscious of these initially subtle perceptions in our everyday lives, the more we come to trust that our own experiences, perceptions, and dreams are valid.

For this reason, it's important to be relaxed about the process of reading the cards. Moments in which our memory falters as to the meaning of a card can actually be the opening we need for intuition to come through. Memorizing the card definitions is one tool for providing accurate readings, but relying too heavily on memorized definitions can keep us from developing and trusting our intuitive understanding of the message. Spend time connecting with your intuitive reaction to a card before you check its meaning in the book.

Kabbalah, numerology, and alchemy, as well as still more spiritual traditions that have found parallels and connections with the tarot, including crystal healing and Ayurveda (the traditional system of medicine in India).

Archetypes and Symbolism

The images of the tarot evoke memories, feelings, questions, and intuitive knowledge; they lead us inward in order to perceive and express truths about our outer world. As a tool for doing so, the characters and situations portrayed by the cards are easy to recognize in our daily lives.

The Magician may be your resourceful friend who makes things happen. The King of Swords might be a strict boss. The Wheel of Fortune shows the way fate can change overnight. Swiss psychiatrist Carl Jung acknowledged the tarot as having "its origin and anticipation in profound patterns of the collective unconscious with access to potentials of increased awareness uniquely at the disposal of these patterns," writes Laurens van der Post in his introduction to Sallie Nichols's book, *Jung and Tarot*. The images in the tarot deck also include the universally important natural elements of air, fire, water, and earth.

The symbols in the tarot deck come from Catholicism and Judaism, as well as Greek and Egyptian mythology. While these traditions have been appropriated into the tarot so that important context has been lost, the symbols and images hold meaning that, if not always entirely universal, are still recognizable to millions of people. Sometimes culturally specific images resonate in our psyches because they express an underlying universality; other times, it is because the influence of that culture is vast and deeply imbued in the ways we understand the world.

Because the images in the cards can hold rich webs of association and represent entire areas of our life, a spread of cards can give us a big-picture perspective that would otherwise be difficult to grasp. Any image or feeling that stands out to us when we see a card points to something within ourselves that is in need of attention.

The tarot reveals visible and invisible lines of relatedness between elements of our experience. Our universe is infinitely nuanced, and our experiences, concepts, places and objects so interrelated that meaning is always waiting to pour forth at any chance we give it.

Toward Self-Discovery

The tarot is both ordinary and mysterious—like us. A key to self-discovery lies in the ability to navigate the relationships between the ordinary and the magical: to name our experience, to match abstract concepts with specific events, and to connect the personal with the universal. In the chapters to come, we'll see how we can use the tarot to unlock the meaning in our lives to cultivate self-awareness and personal empowerment.

2

TAROT MECHANICS

THE TAROT DECK IS COMPRISED OF 78 CARDS: 22 Major Arcana cards (also known as trump or key cards) and 56 Minor Arcana cards, which are divided into four suits. In this chapter, we'll familiarize ourselves with the physical aspects of the tarot cards, dig into how to perform readings, and get to know some of the symbolic dimensions of the cards.

CHOOSING & USING YOUR TAROT DECK

Your tarot deck is a portal to your spiritual self, and it is important to treat it as such. This section discusses a few steps you can take to develop your initial connection with your deck, including choosing a deck, preparing it for use, and caring for it throughout your tarot practice.

Selecting a Deck

This book uses the Rider-Waite-Smith (RWS) system of interpretation, as do most books for beginners. However, this does not mean you must use the RWS deck if it doesn't interest or intrigue you. Hundreds of decks have been created that are based on the 78 archetypes of the RWS deck, so choose any deck you feel an affinity for and trust. Though the cards' specific symbols differ among these decks, the overall upright and reversed meanings described in part 2 will match any deck you choose that uses the RWS system of interpretation.

There are also other decks that use different interpretive systems. The card descriptions in this book will not be helpful to you if you choose the Thoth Tarot Deck or Tarot de Marseille, whose card definitions differ from the RWS deck, or any deck with fewer than 78 archetype cards. However, should you choose to use a non-RWS deck, the methods in this book for growing from the tarot, caring for your deck, and so on will still be relevant to your tarot practice.

Preparing Your Deck for Use

Before you perform your first reading with a new deck, first purify and attune to your deck. Once you start using your deck, care for it by keeping it clean, protected when not in use, and cleared of extraneous energy.

PURIFYING YOUR DECK

When you get a new deck, especially if you are not its first owner, you can purify it by doing one of the following:

- Place your deck on a windowsill or outside during a full moon.
- Bury your deck in salt for a few days (first put your deck in a plastic bag, so the cards do not actually touch the salt!).

Many of the tarot decks you come across will use the roman numeral system (I, II, III, IV, etc.) rather than the standardized Arabic numeral system (1, 2, 3, 4, etc.). Throughout this book, I spell out the numbers in the Minor Arcana cards for ease of reading, but because I refer to the Major Arcana cards by name, they are accompanied in this text by their roman numeral designations.

- Burn sage or a smudge stick and hold your deck in the rising smoke.

- Put the 78 cards of your deck in order: The Fool (0) through The World (XXI), then ace through king of each suit. When you have them in order, reshuffle the deck.

You can return to any one of these methods anytime you feel your deck has picked up extra energy that a regular cleansing method (see below) doesn't take care of.

ATTUNING

Forming a connection with your new deck, or *attuning* to it, comes down to treating your cards with respect and doing anything that helps you come to trust your deck and regard it as important and special.

Before you begin readings with your new deck, spend a week adjusting to it. Keep your deck in a special place, such as on your altar (see page 13), or under your pillow, and spend a little time getting to know the cards every day. You can shuffle them and order them if you like, or simply gaze at the images in the cards, intuitively sensing any emotional, mental, or spiritual connections that arise.

REGULAR CLEANSING

Your deck can hold energy from previous readings and from the environments in which those readings took place. Before you do a reading, do a simple ritual to rid the cards of any extraneous energy. Here are two options:

1 Shuffle your cards rhythmically and tap them on the table to release extra energy. You can develop your own rhythm for this.

2 Fan the deck out in your hand, blow softly on the edges, return the deck to a stack in your hand, and knock once on the top of the deck.

Caring for Your Deck

Store your cards in a protective box or bag to keep them clean and free from absorbing extraneous energy. You can also wrap them in a silk cloth or any cloth of a dark color to keep them from picking up any extra energy. The cloth you wrap your cards in can also serve as your reading cloth, which designates your reading space. Natural material is ideal for protecting your deck—such as a wooden box, or silk, cotton, or linen—but what's most important is that you store your cards, regardless of color or material, with a sense of reverence.

COMPONENTS OF A TAROT READING

What are the components of a tarot reading which happen before and after the actual reading of the cards? To do a tarot reading, it's helpful for us to prepare ourselves, our cards, and our space. Afterward, we clear the reading's energy from the cards.

Prepare Your Space and Deck

You might decide to do your readings in front of your altar or somewhere else that feels special. Really, anywhere that feels peaceful and where you can focus without interruption will do perfectly.

Turn off your phone. If you'd like, light a candle or play music to help you relax and open yourself. You might also invite the guidance of any higher power, asking for perspective or guidance that serves the greatest good. Set the intention or ask for the courage to be open to the wisdom and insight that arrive during the reading, fears and preferences aside. Being consistent with your ritual will help you regularly access a spiritual or associative state in which you relate to ideas and images.

Cleanse your cards (see previous page), then on a clean surface, lay down your reading cloth, if you have one.

Prepare Your Mind

Sit quietly and focus on your breathing for 5 to 10 minutes before doing a reading for yourself. You may find it helpful to visualize a beam of light entering through the top of your head, filling your body with light and continuing into the earth as roots of light, grounding you. Or simply allow your mind to settle on your breathing so that extraneous thoughts fall away or become less urgent, allowing you to open to your inner experience.

What Is an Altar?

An altar is a small table or surface where you keep items of personal spiritual importance. These may include small religious statues, photographs of ancestors, and/or other items that are personally meaningful. An altar may also include items to represent each of the four elements. If you have an altar, or decide to make one, you may wish to keep your tarot cards on your altar. You might meditate or pray in front of your altar, as well as perform tarot readings.

State Your Question

The tarot does not answer yes-or-no questions such as "Is she *the one*?" or "Should I quit my job?" Rather, the cards illuminate present and past dynamics, point to factors we may have overlooked, point to areas in which we need to grow, and can show us the likely future outcomes of our actions—that is, if we continue to proceed on our current path.

The future is not written in stone. We can always choose to change our fate by getting creative with what we have to work with—for example, by cultivating helpful qualities like kindness, curiosity, and resilience, and by becoming more self-aware and deliberate in our decision-making.

Tarot Symbolism

THE LOVERS.

THE DEVIL.

The symbols in the tarot deck come from a variety of mythological and religious lineages. Though they exist apart from the traditions and religions that inspired their imagery, the ideas and archetypes they contain can still resonate in our psyches and offer us relevant insight and guidance, regardless of which traditions we may or may not identify with.

Images from Christian mythology are very present in the Rider-Waite-Smith deck. Adam and Eve appear multiple times, as The Lovers and as the prisoners of The Devil, and we see the snake appear in the Seven of Cups as a symbol of temptation.

We also see the practice of the Christian faith in the landscape of many of the cards, such as churches, and in the vocation of many of the figures, such as The Hierophant (featuring a pope and two monks) or the cathedral stonemason, bishop, and monk in the Three of Pentacles. I find it important to note the influence of Christian symbolism on the definitions of the symbolism of colors in the cards. The emotional and symbolic meanings of various colors vary from culture to culture; the Rider-Waite-Smith deck reveals the limitations of this in its descriptions of the color white as purity and innocence, as it is difficult to escape the racial overtones of this symbolism.

Egyptian mythology—or, rather, European interpretation of Egyptian mythology—also informs the symbolism of many cards. The Star, for example, features an ibis, representing the deity Thoth. We see the ankh, the Egyptian symbol of life, in The Emperor's scepter.

We can also recognize figures from Greek mythology in the imagery of the cards. Persephone's pomegranates adorn The High Priestess's veil and The Empress's dress. The winged helmet and boots of Hermes help propel the Knight of Cups in matters of communication.

Symbolism from the Kabbalah enriches the cards of the tarot, as well. We see the pentacles arranged in the shape of the Tree of Life in the Ten of Pentacles, and the Tree of Life itself suspends The Hanged Man.

Each sign of the zodiac is associated with a Major Arcana card, and other astrological links in the meanings of each card are evident. We also see the glyphs of the zodiac embroidered on the clothing of figures in cards such as The Chariot and the Nine of Swords. Further, alchemical symbols denoting the elements adorn cards such as the Wheel of Fortune. Symbols from other Western occult traditions also appear throughout the deck, such as the Rosicrucian rose in the Death card and the Two of Wands.

When we sit down to do a reading, we might ask questions like:

- What are the most important dynamics at play in my situation?
- What would be the impact of my decision?
- What should I focus on to resolve this issue?
- What quality should I cultivate to best deal with this situation?
- What am I not seeing or refusing to see?
- What issue underlies my situation?
- What are my options in this situation?

If you don't have a burning question, ask something along the lines of, "What influences and possibilities should I be aware of today?" or "What qualities are most relevant for me to cultivate today?"

Choose a spread that suits your question. For some basic spread options and when might be best to use them, see chapter 3.

When you are ready to ask the cards your question, you can ask it aloud, silently in your mind, or write it down in your journal. You may like to keep a special journal especially for recording your tarot readings, including questions, cards, and your interpretations and reflections.

Shuffle

There are many methods for shuffling and cutting the deck. How you mix your deck and choose cards is up to you. What's important is that you allow yourself to be present and open while shuffling and choosing cards. Let your nondominant hand lead, as intuition is said to flow more freely through the nondominant hand than through the more active hand.

The traditional method of shuffling is to pick up the deck, take out a portion of cards from the bottom, and place them on top. Continue to do this until you intuitively feel that the deck is ready. If you would like to cut the deck, use your nondominant hand to divide the deck into two to four stacks, then pile the stacks back together in any order that feels right.

Alternately, you can spread the cards out on your reading cloth or a clean surface and mix them using your nondominant hand. Then, still using your nondominant hand, pull the card or cards you will use for your reading.

In a spread, you can choose to either lay all the cards down, then turn them over one by one, or, to lay the spread face up, and begin by reading either the card that stands out to you or by noticing the connections between the cards, such as multiple aces, a repeated symbol, or cards that seem to contrast each other.

When a card pops out of the deck while you are shuffling, it is significant. If you are doing a One-Card Pull (see page 32), use this card. If you are laying a spread, note the card that jumped out, return it to the deck, and continue to shuffle. Often, this card will reappear in your spread. If it does, pay special attention to its meaning and placement. If it does not, simply keep it in mind during your reading as a guiding element or important supporting factor.

Read the Cards

Learning to connect the symbols in the cards to the events and people in our lives takes practice. This is both an intellectual skill and an intuitive one. In reading tarot, we connect the abstract to the personal. Remember that many factors are at play in this.

When our conscious mind is too hungry for a particular answer, it can mask the messages that our intuition has for us. On the other hand, when we insist that the tarot reading be entirely mystical, we can miss the obvious card meanings staring us in the face. So, allow for a dance to play out between your intuitive and conscious interpretation of the cards. And be patient with yourself and the cards. The epiphany might not happen during the tarot reading, but rather at an unexpected moment in your life, thanks to questions that a reading opened up. Expect each reading to be different.

Chapter 4 offers a step-by-step method for reading the cards for personal growth and empowerment, along with exercises that accompany each step. Overall, my method for reading the cards is a four-part process:

1 Open to your intuitive associations sparked by the cards.

2 Note how your associations and intuitive messages match up with the meanings of the cards.

3 Explore and develop any insight that has come to you through matching the cards' abstract symbols and archetypes with your own experience. Integrate this insight with the conscious way you regard your situation. You can do this through any form of expression such as art, journaling, or simply having a conversation with a trusted friend.

4 Now that this insight has become a conscious part of your thinking, consider what actions your insight compels you to take. Acting in alignment with your insight allows you to express and embody your growth, for the benefit of yourself and everyone you affect.

SPIRITUAL ASSOCIATIONS

The tarot is tied to many spiritual practices, such as astrology, Kabbalah, numerology, and alchemy. Let's take a look at how these aspects can further influence a tarot reading.

Astrology

Systems of overlaying astrology with the tarot have continued to develop since occultists of the Hermetic Order of the Golden Dawn created initial systems for linking these two divinatory systems. Chapter 5 lists the planet or zodiac sign that each Major Arcana card is associated with, but if you are a fan of astrology, there are many books that bring further astrological associations to all 78 cards of the tarot.

What is known about a zodiac sign or a planet in general—or in your astrological chart specifically—provides more clues for interpreting the card. For example, The Empress is associated with the planet Venus. Therefore, the qualities associated with Venus, such as beauty, love, and pleasure, help us get to know The Empress and what she values. Furthermore, if The Empress comes up in a reading, you can look at the position of Venus in your astrological chart to further contextualize and reveal the importance of The Empress qualities in your life right now.

Kabbalah

Kabbalah, the secret oral law said to have been given to Moses in addition to the Torah, is a tradition of Jewish mysticism. It became a foundational influence in the Western occult tradition of Hermetic Qabalah, which blends traditions such as Western astrology, alchemy, Neoplatonism, Gnosticism, and many other influences. As such, it underlies the philosophy of the Tarot as laid out by English occultist A. E. Waite of the Rider-Waite-Smith deck.

Central to the Kabbalah is the Tree of Life. Simplistically put, the Tree of Life offers a map of all experience, material and divine. This map shows us the interconnectedness of all life and details connections between the human and the divine.

The Tree of Life consists of 10 spheres (the sephiroth), each representing an aspect of experience, and 22 pathways connecting them. In the mid-nineteenth century, the French occultist Éliphas Lévi created an extensive system linking elements of the Kabbalah with the Major and Minor Arcana. Among the links he made was matching the 22 Tree of Life pathways to the 22 Major Arcana cards. He also used Kabbalah to reinforce the association of each suit of the Minor Arcana with a natural element: water for cups, fire for wands, earth for pentacles, and air for swords.

The tarot card descriptions in this book do not go into detail about the Hebrew letters or overtly name Kabbalistic concepts as such. However, many Kabbalistic concepts have become incorporated into the standard definitions of the cards.

Numerology

Numerology, the study of the meaning of numbers, reveals to us significant facets of each card. For example, 3 is a number of creation (as in two forces combining to form a third thing, such as two parents and a child) and balance (as in the geometric stability of a triangle). The numerological significance of each tarot card is discussed i n part 2 of this book.

Rosicrucianism

This Protestant-based, Kabbalah-inspired occult order begun in early 15th century Germany by medical doctors whose vows included healing the sick free of charge. The Rosicrucians' focus included philosophy, science, meditation, telepathy, and alchemy.

Rosicrucianism laid a foundation for The Hermetic Order of the Golden Dawn (founded in 1888), the esoteric order from which sprang modern-day tarot cards. In the tarot, we see the symbol of Rosicrucianism, the Rosy Cross, on cards such as Death and the Two of Wands. In this symbol, the cross signifies the human body and the rose symbolizes consciousness blossoming forth from the body.

Alchemy

Alchemists not only sought to turn lead into gold but also aimed to transform their own human imperfections that weighed them down, burning off their flaws to unite with the divine.

An early link between alchemy and the tarot appears in the Visconti-Sforza deck in the fifteenth century, in which The Hermit portrays an alchemist at work in his laboratory. As alchemy flourished in the seventeenth and eighteenth centuries, along with occultism and the divinatory uses of the tarot, decks for the by-then-popular game of tarot began bearing alchemical symbols in their cards, which became part of divinatory interpretations of the cards. You will see this in many cards, but especially in the Wheel of Fortune, which features at its center the alchemical symbols for mercury, sulfur, water, and salt—the four alchemical foundational elements of life.

THE MAJOR ARCANA

The word *arcana* means "mystery." The Major Arcana—the 22 key cards or trump cards—are the "major mysteries" of life. The Major Arcana cards show up in a reading when we're willing to go deep—or when life has forced us to go deep. In times of fundamental change, upheaval, or growth, such as grief, a career path shift, or falling in love, the Major Arcana guides us.

The Major Arcana is also referred to as the Fool's Journey. The Fool (card 0) represents the *querent*, the adventure-seeker within each of us who traverses the path of the cards 1 through 21. The journey of the Major Arcana can be visually mapped out as three rows of seven, called *septenaries*. Each septenary represents a level of development: conscious, unconscious, and higher consciousness. For further reading about this, Rachel Pollack's books, specifically *Seventy-Eight Degrees of Wisdom: A Book of Tarot*, offer thorough interpretations of the Fool's Journey.

THE EMPRESS.

THE EMPEROR.

THE HIEROPHANT.

THE LOVERS.

THE CHARIOT.

WHEEL of FORTUNE.

JUSTICE.

THE HANGED MAN.

DEATH.

TEMPERANCE.

THE STAR.

THE MOON.

THE SUN.

JUDGEMENT.

THE WORLD.

THE MINOR ARCANA

While the Major Arcana represent major shifts, powerful influences, and soul-level growth, the Minor Arcana cards indicate specific facets of everyday life. These are the "minor mysteries" of life. The Minor Arcana cards illuminate situations and influences which are temporary or relatively superficial compared to the Major Arcana cards.

There are four suits in the Minor Arcana: Cups, Pentacles, Swords, and Wands. Each suit is comprised of 10 number cards and four court cards: Pages, Knights, Queens, Kings.

The four suits of the Minor Arcana map our experience into four different spheres or qualities of energy. Each suit is associated with a natural element to further elucidate the qualities of the suit.

 The suit of CUPS is associated with the element of water. The Cup cards address matters of emotions, relationships, inner life, and spirituality.

 PENTACLES, associated with the element of earth, represent the physical world, raw material, the body, health, resources, money, and career.

 The air element is attributed to the suit of SWORDS. Swords represent critical thinking, clarity, and mind-sets.

The socially oriented WANDS are the fire element. They represent activity, creativity, vision, communication, and enterprise. The Wand cards help us understand our active role and purpose within groups—family, workplace, and community.

Each number carries a common meaning across the four suits:

ONE (ACE) Oneness, Beginnings, Power

TWO Duality, Balance, Choice, Partnership

THREE Synthesis, Creativity, Dynamic Balance

FOUR Material Achievement, Structure, Order

FIVE Change, Challenge, Uncertainty, Mediation

SIX Harmony, Integration, Passivity

SEVEN Spirituality, Tests

EIGHT Navigation, Prosperity, Authority

NINE Completion, Meditation, Achievement of Goals

TEN Pinnacle (of Success or Difficulty), Beginnings and Endings

While numbers 1 to 10 represent situations, the court cards represent people and personality traits:

PAGES are beginners, students, young people, and apprentices. They are inspired and curious.

KNIGHTS are skilled in the realm of their particular suit, though they do not entirely understand their path, nor have they mastered it. They are often more gung ho and passionate than they are discerning. They are determined to save the world, pursue ideas, build great things, and fall in love.

QUEENS represent inner mastery. The queens help others cultivate the qualities of their suit within themselves, as well.

KINGS represent external mastery and leadership. Self-reliance characterizes their expression of competence in the qualities of their suit.

Putting It Together

Learning the qualities of these suits, along with the significance of each number or court personality, gives you all the information you need to begin reading the Minor Arcana cards on your own. For example, let's look at the Four of Wands.

To ascertain the basic meaning of this card, all we need to know is that fours represent the achievement of stability and order, and wands represent the social realm. What does stability in the social realm look like? The attainment of a stable role in one's family, community, or job—such as marriage, winning an election or receiving a promotion, becoming a soccer coach, or getting tenure.

PREPARING FOR GROWTH

This book is intended to support you as you connect with your intuition, understand and express your insight, and integrate your insight into your perceptions and actions. The tarot can offer perspective and insight for growth in all areas of life, from relationships, career decisions, and creative projects to home life and spiritual questions. The cards help us become more self-aware, understanding, generous, and compassionate. They support us in making decisions, exploring our experience, being creative, and taking actions that allow us to live fulfilling lives of beauty, passion, connection, and integrity.

Card Spreads

Tarot card spreads allow us to view multiple aspects of a question or situation at once and their connections. The positioning of each card in a tarot spread helps define the meaning of that card, and each card represents a facet of your experience. These facets can be anything from "influences from the recent past" to "how I see myself" to "my heart in my relationship" to "what I need to let go of."

By showing us many facets of our life at once, spreads allow us to zoom out and get a big-picture look at our lives or at a particular situation. Looking at various facets of our lives at once also allows us to easily make connections we may otherwise overlook, as well as settle into the meaning in our lives, and understand our lives as journeys, as opposed to judging ourselves according to how well we succeed or fail at fitting into external definitions of failure or success.

One important aspect of reading a spread is reversals (upside-down cards). Reversals rarely represent the opposite of a card's upright meaning. Rather, they can indicate:

- **An extreme quality or circumstance** (usually negative, but not always) of that card, such as the confidence of the King of Wands becoming egotism when the card is reversed.
- **The upright meaning, but with added difficulties, delay, or resistance.** The upright qualities are latent in our situation or in our attitude.
- **Emphasis on the upright meaning.** Occasionally, a card appears reversed as a way to get us to pay attention to it.

- **The circumstance indicated by the upright card has now ended,**
especially if the upright card describes a painful circumstance. For
example, the indecision of the Two of Swords is resolved with a decision
or the mourner in the Five of Cups emerges from a period of grief.

How do you know which of the above options is the case? Go with your
intuition. You'll be able to tell, for example, whether The Sun is reversed
because you're feeling unnecessarily gloomy or because you're outright
ecstatic. The card descriptions in part 2 also give guidance on the
reversed meaning of each card. It's important to remember not to lose
hope when you see a card come up in reverse. Sometimes just seeing a
card in the reversed position is enough to jar us into a realization about
what the problem is and how to solve it.

The cards illuminate one another, creating the overall message in a
variety of ways. For one, when a quality is held in common by two or more
cards, such as a repeated suit, number, or theme (for example, balance,
beginnings, or endings), that quality is emphasized in the overall message
of the spread.

Conversely, cards can reveal the dynamics or tensions of a situation
when their qualities oppose or add complexities to one another, such as
when the Eight of Cups shows us leaving home to travel indefinitely, while
the Four of Pentacles reveals a need to secure our resources. This might
indicate a complicated truth about our needs, desires, priorities, and
worldview.

Finally, cards create a narrative, or plot arc, by showing past, present,
and future (beginning, middle, and end) as well as our motivations and
the important people, places, communities, and ideas in our lives.

A Beginner's Reading

To interpret this sample spread or any other spread, combine the meaning of each card with the meaning of its placement. Notice how these meanings describe your life, and look for the narrative that emerges, which relates these elements of your life to one another and allows you to make sense of all the information. In chapter 3, you'll find a number of common spreads and sample readings. For our first reading, let's choose the Past/Present/Future spread and use Imani's experience as an example to uncover the narrative:

Imani is a recent college grad who feels the need to be more connected to community, but she isn't sure which of her communities she should focus on forming deeper connections with (family, friends, work, neighborhood, or political). She wonders which considerations or themes should guide her. She decides to do a Past/Present/Future spread to get a general sense of her path.

IMANI'S CARDS:

1   2   3

POSITION 1 Past Situation and Influences—Two of Wands

POSITION 2 Present Situation and Influences—Nine of Cups

POSITION 3 Future Situation and Influences—Seven of Wands

IMANI'S FIRST CARD: THE TWO OF WANDS

This is in the Past Situation and Influences position. It's a card of active, creative partnership, something Imani has always valued—she's always had a best friend or romantic partner. This card in this position helps Imani to find a meaningful point of growth to go out on her own more often.

IMANI'S SECOND CARD: THE NINE OF CUPS

Imani's Present Situation and Influences card portrays a generous host. It encourages Imani to reflect on the gatherings of family and friends already taking place in her life. Occasionally, Imani hosts storytelling potlucks in her home for her friends, family, and neighbors. The Nine of Cups encourages her to keep bringing people together like this and focus on making it a regular priority.

IMANI'S THIRD CARD: THE SEVEN OF WANDS

This is a card of defending yourself and others, as guided by your beliefs. Due to the card's position of Future Situation and Influences, if Imani continues on her current path, she can expect to get in touch with a greater sense of conviction through hosting her community events. She will likely find herself standing up for something she believes in.

Overall, Imani is ready to take initiative in hosting the people and gatherings she cares about. Through doing this, she'll tap into conviction and community support that will bring her to a point of defending what matters to her and, likely, to her community.

HOW TO USE THIS BOOK

Now that you have some background knowledge on the tarot and have a general idea of how to interpret tarot cards for personal insight and growth, the remainder of this book is designed to guide you through the process of building a strong relationship with the cards, as well as with your own intuition, in order to consistently access the tarot's guidance.

In chapter 3, you will find a number of common spreads and suggestions on how to use them. The method I share in chapter 4 will help you gain deeper awareness of your experiences through meditating on the cards. This method assists you in finding the meaning of each tarot spread you lay for yourself.

Each of the 78 cards is explored in detail in part 2 of this book. Refer to the card definitions during the interpretation process, but keep in mind that your connection with the cards is as important as the meanings of the cards themselves.

You can learn the cards *quickly* by studying their definitions. You can learn the cards *thoroughly* by doing readings, building your understanding of the profound and nuanced types of experience each card represents. To learn to use the cards most effectively, I recommend a combination of reading the cards for yourself (using the spreads in chapter 3 and the exercises in chapter 4) and setting aside a little time every day or every week to commit the definitions in part 2 to memory.

3

COMMON
CARD SPREADS &
SAMPLE READINGS

IN THIS CHAPTER, we'll dig into the practice of reading the cards by exploring 10 of the most fundamental card spreads and sample readings. While specific sample readings are offered in this chapter, the spreads are applicable to an array of topics and questions.

After you have prepared yourself and your cards as described in chapter 2, you can choose your spread according to the type of insight you seek and the scope of perspective you need. For example, decision-making is helped along by the Comparing Your Options spread, and spiritual growth is aided by the Let Go/Grow spread. The One-Card Pull offers perspective on a single issue or guidance for your day or your week, while the Celtic Cross spread and the Essential Keys spread offer perspective that spans a longer stretch of time and likely encompasses more areas of your life (though even a One-Card Pull may have far-reaching insight). Ultimately, when choosing which spread to use, just do what feels right.

The Significator

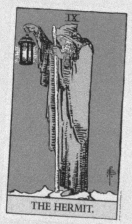

THE HERMIT.

THE WORLD.

The significator card, commonly referred to as the signifier card, is a card that is predesignated (rather than pulled from the deck) to represent you, the Seeker. It is intended to personalize your reading and narrow the scope of the reading to channel information that is most relevant to you. This card can be useful if your spreads are feeling impersonal and difficult to connect to.

I personally do not use signifier cards because I am more interested in the different, often unexpected facets of ourselves that come to the surface on any given day or in any given moment. While some readers use a signifier card to add coherence to a reading, I embrace the variations and fluctuations in our personality and state of being that are revealed without this card. Reading without a signifier card also frees up that card to show up in other placements within the spread. Neither way is correct or incorrect. It's a matter of preference.

I have not included instructions for using a signifier card in the spread descriptions or sample readings in this book. However, if you find it helpful to use a signifier card or wish to try it out, here are some simple instructions for integrating the use of a signifier card into your practice:

In many traditions, the signifier card is identified based on your gender and complexion. This is very obviously a racist, sexist, and gender-normative technique. A less problematic technique is to choose the signifier card according to the court card that corresponds to your age and astrological sun sign. However, I find this technique overly limiting, as our sun sign and age never paint a full picture of our motivations or experience.

My preferred method is to designate a seeker's signifier card as their Life Path Major Arcana card, as I find the Major Arcana cards to be more resonant and full of profound possibilities. To choose your signifier card, follow the instructions in the Life Path spread (see page 38) for calculating your Life Path card, and use that card as your signifier.

To use the signifier in a reading, first lay the signifier face up on the table. Then, lay the first card of the spread crosswise on top of the signifier card. If you use a signifier card in the Celtic Cross spread, place your predesignated signifier card in Position 1, then draw cards from the deck to lay in Positions 2 to 10. Read this card by noting any correlations between its imagery and/or meaning and that of any of the other cards in the spread.

ONE-CARD PULL

Simply pull one card from the deck and lay it in front of you on your reading cloth or table. One tarot card often yields more than enough inspiration to satisfy ordinary queries. Additionally, you can pull a card every morning for information about what to focus on during the day.

I generally pull a card for myself at the beginning of every week as a way of getting in touch with the themes and questions to explore for the next seven days. The card I pull always helps me make sense of the events in my life, connect more meaningfully, and know which opportunities to accept or say, "No, thank you" to.

Sometimes the card confirms my hunches or intuition about a situation. Other times, the card pushes me to move outside my comfort zone, showing me ways in which I've been acting out of fear or an unconscious habit. Still other times, the card reveals a glimpse of the bigger picture when my focus is too narrow, brings me back to the task at hand when I'm distracted, or surprises me with an entirely new way of seeing my situation. I always find meaning in inhabiting the questions, themes, and qualities of a card, uncovering the textures of its meanings and adding my own experiential associations to my understanding of the card.

1

Sample One-Card Pull

Aarti is a busy, middle-aged professional. Amidst her many responsibilities, she doesn't want to lose sight of keeping healthy. She asks her cards, "What should I be aware of with regard to my health?" While the tarot should never be consulted in lieu of a medical professional, the cards can provide additional reminders and inspiration for respecting and connecting with our bodies.

1

POSITION 1 The World

Aarti shuffles the deck and pulls THE WORLD.

The World is a card of completion. Aarti should bring to completion any projects in her life that have been dragged out, so that she doesn't allow loose ends and unresolved conflicts to stress and distract her from what makes her feel alive.

Because The World is also a card of celebration and joy, it suggests that Aarti will do well to celebrate her good health. She should do activities that make her happy and bring her joy. She should dance.

Aarti will be celebrating her birthday next month. The World inspires her to complete her hanging projects before her birthday so that she can celebrate with a worry-free mind, thus restoring the role of joy and celebration into the balance of her health and lifestyle.

LET GO/GROW

When we feel blocked, but don't know why, the Let Go/Grow spread fuels us with insight and direction. It helps us accept challenges and move through transitions more gracefully.

1   **2**

POSITION 1 What I Need to Let Go

POSITION 2 Quality to Focus on for Growth

Sample Let Go/Grow Reading

Astrid comes to the cards wondering how she should seek out passion (both romantic and intellectual) in safe ways and places. She asks, "What's blocking me that I need to let go of? And what quality will help me live a life that is passionate, but not destructive?"

1   2

The **EIGHT OF CUPS** suggests that Astrid needs to let go of some of her wanderlust. The Eight of Cups is a card of leaving one's well-ordered life to seek fulfillment elsewhere. Astrid has been living a life of perpetual leaving. She travels often and enjoys dating outside of her primary partnership. When she sees the Eight of Cups in the position of what she needs to let go, she sees that while her adventures have helped her grow in the past, her pattern of leaving constantly takes her away from the meaningful, and potentially more passionate, life she does have.

How might she channel her wandering energy into her present life with her partner Stephanie? The **SEVEN OF CUPS** is a card of creativity. What possibilities can she dream up with Stephanie (as opposed to her solo adventures)? What can they imagine or explore together?

Stephanie and Astrid have long been dreaming of expanding their farm to include a rescue animal sanctuary. Astrid knows that realizing this dream together would be a meaningful and fulfilling adventure that would make her feel more alive and more connected to herself, to her partner, and to the role she wants to play in the world. She sets the intention to let go of her habit of leaving and instead grow into the possibilities of the life she and Stephanie have dreamed for themselves.

PAST/PRESENT/FUTURE

The Past/Present/Future spread is a simple way to arrange some of the chaos of our life into a meaningful narrative, giving us a window into how we've grown and what our direction, values, or goals are now.

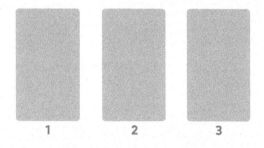

1   2   3

POSITION 1 Past Situation and Influences

POSITION 2 Present Situation and Influences

POSITION 3 Future Situation and Influences

Sample Past/Present/Future Reading

Alex's son Dylan is about to enter high school. Alex goes to his tarot deck for guidance on how to best parent his son at this time. He chooses the Past/Present/Future spread to reflect on how he has been able to support Dylan's growth in the past, and what might need to change in his parenting style now to best support Dylan during his high school years.

ACE of SWORDS. WHEEL of FORTUNE. ACE of WANDS.

1   2   3

POSITION 1 Ace of Swords

POSITION 2 Wheel of Fortune

POSITION 3 Ace of Wands

In position 1, Past Situation and Influences, the ACE OF SWORDS indicates the intelligence and success of Alex's parenting method during his son's childhood. As a new parent, Alex read many parenting books and was very intellectually diligent about his parenting methods. The Ace of Swords focuses on writing, publishing, the intellect, and success. Alex and his wife were successful in raising a smart and happy child.

In position 2, Present Situation and Influences, the WHEEL OF FORTUNE—which represents a change of fate—refers to Alex and his wife's divorce when Dylan was in middle school. This change was difficult for the family to adjust to. Alex did not find parenting books about divorce to be helpful, so instead he has been parenting with a day-by-day method of responding to issues as they arise and adjusting his style to his family's new life and to his growing and changing child.

In position 3, Future Situation and Influences, we see another Ace. This time, it is the ACE OF WANDS. Though Dylan's life during middle school was a time of upheaval and change, Alex and his son will soon get to experience another time marked by the potential, energy, and success of an Ace. As this period of major change wraps up, and Dylan's and Alex's energy is no longer so engaged in getting through each day, new energy brings new possibilities. The Ace of Wands is a card of family and social engagement. Alex will do well to focus on engaging Dylan in father-son activities and supporting Dylan to have a positive social life. The possibilities will soon reveal themselves.

LIFE PATH

The Life Path spread uses numerology to identify some of the guiding archetypes in your life. Using only the Major Arcana, this spread offers a big-picture perspective on where you have been, where you are now, and where you may be headed.

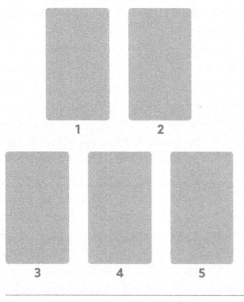

POSITION 1	Life Path
POSITION 2	Shadow
POSITION 3	Past Year
POSITION 4	Present Year
POSITION 5	Next Year

Calculate your LIFE PATH CARD by adding up the digits of your month, day, and year of birth. For example, if you were born on January 3, 1989, do the following calculation: 1+3+1+9+8+9=31. If this sum is a double-digit number, add together the digits until you arrive at a single-digit sum. For example, 3+1=4. Your Life Path Card would be IV. The Emperor.

Next, use the following chart to calculate your SHADOW CARD. A shadow is an unconscious personality trait that, when it remains unconscious, can drive us into trouble and create inner struggle, conflict, and confusion.

IF YOUR LIFE PATH CARD IS:	YOUR SHADOW CARD(S) IS:
I. The Magician	X. Wheel of Fortune, XIX. The Sun
II. The High Priestess	XI. Justice, XX. Judgement
III. The Empress	XII. The Hanged Man, XXI. The World
IV. The Emperor	0. The Fool, XIII. Death
V. The Hierophant	XIV. Temperance
VI. The Lovers	XV. The Devil
VII. The Chariot	XVI. The Tower
VIII. Strength	XVII. The Star
IX. The Hermit	XVIII. The Moon

Calculate your PAST YEAR CARD by adding up the digits of the day and month (but not year) of your birth, plus the four digits of the previous year. If necessary, reduce the resulting number by adding together the digits to arrive at a number from 1 to 21. Choose the Major Arcana card that corresponds to that number.

Calculate your PRESENT YEAR CARD by adding up the digits of the day and month of your birth, with the four digits of the current year. If necessary, reduce the resulting number by adding together the digits to arrive at a number from 1 to 21. Choose the Major Arcana card that corresponds to that number.

Calculate your NEXT YEAR CARD by adding up the digits of the day and month of your birth, with the four digits of the year to come. If necessary, reduce the resulting number by adding together the digits to arrive at a number from 1 to 21. Choose the Major Arcana card that corresponds to that number.

Sample Life Path Reading

Kim finds that she has grown a lot in the past year, but she is having trouble putting words to these changes she sees in herself. She also wishes to reflect on how her recent growth fits with the overall path of her life. She lays a Life Path spread to get a deep, big-picture perspective.

1   2

POSITION 1	The Hierophant
POSITION 2	Temperance
POSITION 3	The Hanged Man
POSITION 4	Death
POSITION 5	Temperance

3   4   5

THE HIEROPHANT in the position of Kim's Life Path tells us that Kim's ultimate purpose is to learn, teach, and create meaningful communities that further the possibilities of knowledge that bridges the human and the divine and informs the ways we respect and support one another.

An important facet of The Hierophant's path is learning how to participate in institutions of knowledge without suffering or perpetuating conformist behavior, but rather fostering meaningful discovery alongside the preservation of wisdom.

TEMPERANCE in the Shadow position indicates that Kim's shadow side is her tendency toward indulgence and/or deprivation. As a shadow, Temperance indicates lack of balance, either through hedonism or through deprivation (as in eating disorders or ostracizing our emotions from our conscious experience). However, whatever our shadow side may be, it propels us invisibly and erratically only until we begin to learn the nature of this challenge and accept that the positive side of this trait lies within us. Because we have to learn this trait the hard way, we come to understand all its ins and outs, its many dimensions. In this way, Temperance may become Kim's strongest trait if she embraces its messages.

Representing the previous year, Kim's card is THE HANGED MAN. Lessons came up for her about self-sacrifice, despair, trust, and faith. After wondering whether she would ever be recognized and appreciated for who she is, she decided to live according to her belief and faith in the universe, rather than by the approval or disapproval of others. (Note that we continue to integrate the lessons of any given year through the date of our birthday the following year.)

This year, the DEATH card indicates that Kim's lessons relate to endings, release, and transformation. After coming to the realization last year that she must release both her need for external acknowledgment and her resentment about not receiving it, this year Kim actually goes through the process of releasing her previous attitudes about acknowledgment. The pain in this growth is that she has had to face her strong fear of rejection. The transformation is that she has not allowed her fear of rejection to stop her, the way it has in the past. This has allowed her to actually better embrace her life path, The Hierophant, as she feels more confident in her ability to participate in institutions without being either rejected or falling into conformity.

Next year is an important year for Kim, as the card of her coming year, TEMPERANCE, is also her shadow side. Kim will learn much about what it means to have balance in her life. Temperance is a card of flourishing emotionally, creatively, and spiritually, due to having all the necessary elements in the right balance. Kim's Temperance year will likely be a year in which the pain of The Hanged Man and of Death transform themselves into art, community, and love.

ESSENTIAL KEYS

The Essential Keys spread allows us to zoom out and get a quick snapshot of our life. This spread gives us a glimpse of past, present, and future, while also focusing on our abilities and passions. This spread comes from Benebell Wen's book, *Holistic Tarot*.

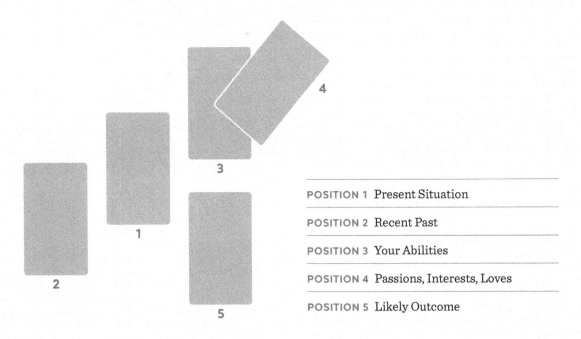

POSITION 1 Present Situation

POSITION 2 Recent Past

POSITION 3 Your Abilities

POSITION 4 Passions, Interests, Loves

POSITION 5 Likely Outcome

Sample Essential Keys Reading

As part of their regular reflective practice, Larry gives themself an Essential Keys reading.

POSITION 1	Nine of Wands
POSITION 2	Eight of Wands
POSITION 3	Seven of Wands
POSITION 4	The Tower
POSITION 5	Page of Cups

The **NINE OF WANDS** in the position of Larry's Present Situation indicates defensiveness. Larry recently moved in with their partner and has been finding that their communication style isn't working. Larry is used to preemptively defending their point of view to their partners and communicating defensively. However, Larry's current partner, Jay, is taken aback by this communication style and would rather discuss issues more gently. At the same time, Larry feels defensive about their new home with Jay. They are building a nourishing relationship and home together, and Larry is on the lookout for anything that could threaten their life together.

The **EIGHT OF WANDS** in the position of the Recent Past shows a clear progression from Eight to Nine of Wands. For the past three years, Larry's living situation was constantly up in the air. It was often disrupted, and they moved constantly. The Eight of Wands indicates, in addition to travel, a flurry of activity that constitutes a final push to success. Larry was able to go from an unstable role in work and community to landing a job and home that is worthy of protecting.

The **SEVEN OF WANDS** in the position of Larry's Abilities shows us the positive light of Larry's communication style and the role they take in their communities, family, and job: Larry stands up for their values. While their communication within their relationship may currently err on the side of being disproportionately defensive, in general Larry is a compassionate and assertive communicator who defends themself and others against injustices. In their work as a nanny, Larry teaches children to communicate in compassionate and community-minded ways. Larry can tap into their talent for effective and compassionate communication to improve their connection with their partner, Jay.

THE TOWER may at first seem a surprising card to appear in the position of Passions, Interests, and Loves. However, to Larry, this card makes sense. Larry loves destroying capitalism, patriarchy, and gender binaries. After nearly taking their own life a number of years ago, they made a commitment to themself. Rather than choosing self-destructive actions, they would instead channel their power of destruction at institutions of oppression. They are emphatic about undercutting violence in their communities, for the health, happiness, and safety of everyone. Larry understands The Tower—their compassionate use of destruction—to be a connecting theme throughout their actions.

In the position of Larry's Likely Outcome, the **PAGE OF CUPS** indicates that Larry and Jay will succeed in creating a safe home and a harmonious relationship that allows for a spirit of sweetness, creativity, and the discovery of new feelings.

CELTIC CROSS

The Celtic Cross is one of the most well-known tarot spreads. It offers a nuanced look at a situation. You can choose to use this spread for a general life reading or to examine at the factors in any given situation, such as career or spiritual growth.

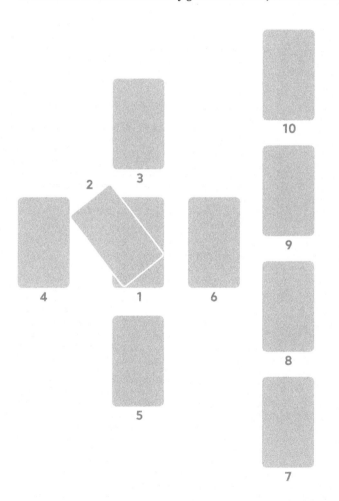

POSITION 1	Seeker's Current State
POSITION 2	Tensions, Obstacles, Additional Energies
POSITION 3	Foundation or Subconscious Influence
POSITION 4	Past Influences on the Present
POSITION 5	Top of Mind Considerations and Aspirations
POSITION 6	Near Future
POSITION 7	How Seeker Sees Themself, Qualities Seeker Brings to the Situation
POSITION 8	Environmental and Social Influences
POSITION 9	Hopes and Fears
POSITION 10	Likely Outcome

Sample Celtic Cross Reading

Lucía just turned 28. As her early adulthood comes to a close, she would like to find perspective about where she stands in life. What needs to be celebrated? What could use extra attention? Are the areas of her life in balance? What are her best next steps?

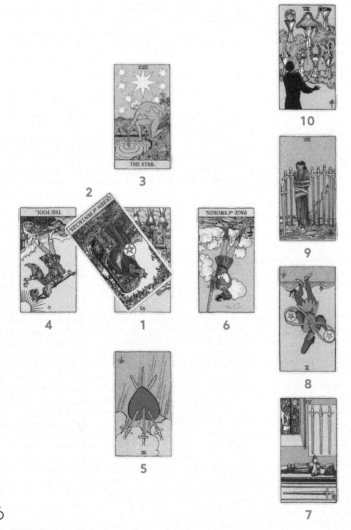

POSITION 1	Six of Cups, Reversed
POSITION 2	Queen of Pentacles, Reversed
POSITION 3	The Star
POSITION 4	The Fool, Reversed
POSITION 5	Three of Swords, Reversed
POSITION 6	Page of Swords, Reversed
POSITION 7	Four of Swords
POSITION 8	Two of Pentacles, Reversed
POSITION 9	Eight of Swords
POSITION 10	Seven of Cups

The SIX OF CUPS, reversed, shows that nostalgia currently overpowers Lucía's perception. What is she nostalgic for? Generally, she aches for more comfortable days in which her basic needs were anticipated and taken care of by her parents. She's also nostalgic for the security of one of her past relationships, in which both she and her partner didn't have to worry as much about income as she does now, and were able to create a cozy home together.

The reversal of the Six of Cups shows, for one thing, that Lucía has been falling into nostalgia's temptation to see her past through rose-colored glasses. The reversal of this card also points to the disruption Lucía feels in her current home-making attempts, as she divides her time between her home in New York City and her partner's home in upstate New York. The discomfort of her current back-and-forth lifestyle might be the cause for her nostalgia. Seeing the Six of Cups, reversed, Lucía realizes how absorbed she has been in her nostalgia, that she has neglected to focus on actual solutions in her present life.

The QUEEN OF PENTACLES, reversed, echoes Lucía's realization about where she's been focusing her attention. Upright, the Queen of Pentacles has a knack for channeling resources to make everyone involved feel grounded and supported. Reversed, the Queen of Pentacles finds herself swept up in other tasks and concerns. This certainly describes Lucía, as she has been channeling her resources into establishing her freelancing career and has not been able to put her resources into a home. She does feel powerless about creating an ideal home, and so is waiting for more resources, including time, to arrive before making decisions or acting.

The tension of cards in positions 1 and 2 shows that while making a home is a current need for Lucía, the resources to support that task are either unavailable, not prioritized, or not being seen. Realizing that this is an issue, Lucía decides to do one small thing each week to establish a feeling of home in her life.

THE STAR in position 3 shows us that hope, inspiration, and renewal are fundamental to understanding Lucía's current situation. Lucía does have big visions for a home life much different from her current situation, involving a creative and tightly woven community in an inspiring location, which makes her desires no easy feat to attain. Additionally, Lucía dreams big in general and could use a home base that feels stable enough to support all the big plans she has for her life. Luckily, the cards in positions 1 and 2 indicate temporary situations, while The Star indicates that her ability to inspire and be inspired are here to stay.

THE FOOL, reversed, suggests foolishness and irresponsibility. The placement of this card in the Past Influences on the Present position shows that Lucía's days of being irresponsible—in many areas of life, as the Major Arcana cards never limit themselves to just one area—are behind her for now.

Top of mind for Lucía is the THREE OF SWORDS, reversed. This indicates upheaval and pain, but at least a chance to vent and release. She and her partner reliably help one another vent and discuss their problems and release emotions. Sharing how she feels with her partner, though difficult as they both feel stress about their living situations, is a priority.

In position 6 is the PAGE OF SWORDS, reversed. Upright, the Page of Swords is a perceiver of power dynamics and relays messages regarding such dynamics. Reversed, he uses his understanding of human psychology to gossip or manipulate.

Seeing this, Lucía warns herself to be discerning about any information she receives in the near future, as it may be inaccurate and intended to manipulate or harm. Especially as her living situation seems to be critical at the moment, she should be discerning about potential roommates and information she receives regarding potential housing. In light of The Star, she must be sure that her inspired visions that lead her are combined with intuition and critical thinking, rather than allowing her gullibility to lead her into a trap. It's important for her to reflect on her foolish actions in the near past (mostly partying too hard) so that they stay in her past and don't resurface as the shadow side of The Star, gullibility, when new information appears that on the surface might seem to help her.

In position 7 is another Swords card. Note that the FOUR OF SWORDS follows the Three of Swords, which is top of mind for Lucía. She sees herself as halted. Her need to express and release pent-up emotions about housing matches her view of herself as preparing mentally for the decisions she is going to need to make about where and how she lives. On the positive side, the energy and perspective she now has from putting her foolish partying days behind her does give her a chance to rest and prepare.

Lucía knows what the TWO OF PENTACLES, reversed, refers to. This is the card of balancing a double life. Living in two places is making her feel out of balance. However, the latent potential for energy and momentum is also present in the upright meaning of this card. Perhaps there is a way for Lucía to harness the potential of her dynamic living situation in a way that allows her to better live the starry visions she has for herself, her partner, and her communities.

The position of the EIGHT OF SWORDS, position 9, reveals hopes or fears. The Eight of Swords is a painful card, so it shows her fear of being trapped by considerations she is not privy to. This resonates with the reversed Page of Swords, which indicates someone using whatever knowledge they have against her. She senses her own lack of awareness about the forces that define her paradigm, and she feels anxiety about not knowing what path to take or even being able to differentiate between paths at all. She fears becoming trapped in her current state of insecurity or accidentally trapping herself in a bad situation.

In position 10, the SEVEN OF CUPS still indicates a plethora of potentially beguiling options in the future, but is a more positive and hopeful card than the Eight of Swords. It also suggests progress from her current Six of Cups, reversed, nostalgia: moving from looking backward to imagining ahead. Amidst fantasies and wishful thinking, the Seven of Cups suggests hope for an imaginative solution. Imaginative solutions are, indeed, one of the only things that release us from Eight of Swords paralysis—and sometimes it takes the pressure of the Eight of Swords to create the stakes for a solution so creative it could not have been casually dreamed up.

Overall at this point in her life, Lucía needs to pay attention to fantasy. She should focus on being in touch with her creativity and optimism, *and* her ability to be discerning about the options presented to her, to steer clear of gullibility or wishful thinking. Shaking off some of her nostalgia will help her clear her vision for this task.

Important next steps for Lucía involve turning her attention toward real progress in improving her home situation. Expressing her emotions about the stress she is experiencing will help her release extra stress and clarify her options. Most important, she should let herself be guided by the positive qualities of The Star, the foundation of this spread, which encourages release and cleansing.

RELATIONSHIP

The relationship spread I like to use follows the same layout as the Celtic Cross, but uses slightly different meanings of the card placements. It can be used for insight into romantic or nonromantic relationships. It is best done with both people present (each person takes one half of the deck, or their own full tarot deck, shuffles, and take turns laying down the cards), but it can also be done alone by one person to gain insight into the dynamics of an important relationship. This spread comes from Mary K. Greer's book *Tarot for Your Self*.

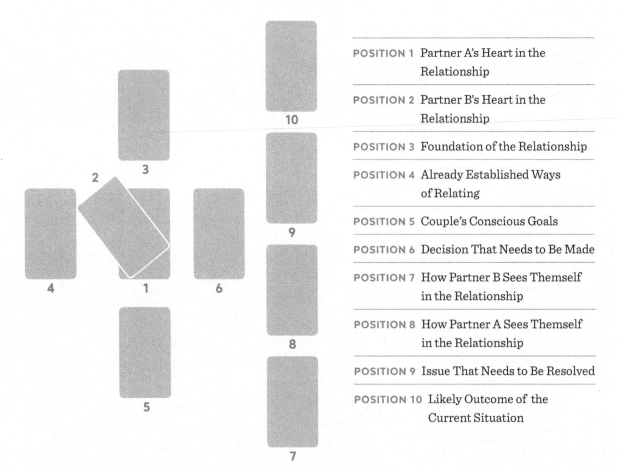

POSITION 1	Partner A's Heart in the Relationship
POSITION 2	Partner B's Heart in the Relationship
POSITION 3	Foundation of the Relationship
POSITION 4	Already Established Ways of Relating
POSITION 5	Couple's Conscious Goals
POSITION 6	Decision That Needs to Be Made
POSITION 7	How Partner B Sees Themself in the Relationship
POSITION 8	How Partner A Sees Themself in the Relationship
POSITION 9	Issue That Needs to Be Resolved
POSITION 10	Likely Outcome of the Current Situation

Sample Relationship Reading

Rachel and Seth have been dating for six months. They lay a Relationship spread to reflect on their partnership.

POSITION 1 Knight of Cups

POSITION 2 Ace of Cups

POSITION 3 Eight of Wands

POSITION 4 Five of Swords

POSITION 5 Temperance, Reversed

POSITION 6 Five of Pentacles

POSITION 7 The World

POSITION 8 Knight of Pentacles

POSITION 9 The Hanged Man, Reversed

POSITION 10 Six of Pentacles

The KNIGHT OF CUPS in the position of Rachel's Heart in the Relationship reveals Rachel's passion and idealism about this love. When a Knight faces another card, it can give us clues about the nature or direction of the Knight's passion. The position of this Knight, facing the FIVE OF PENTACLES, indicates that Rachel may have idealistic ideas about bonding through hardship. The Knight of Cups can get easily hurt or impatient when a person or situation challenges their ideals.

Looking ahead for insight as to where this may come up as an issue, we see the placement of the Five of Pentacles in position 6, Decision That Needs to Be Made. Can Rachel and Seth make decisions together that help them get through a difficult time in which external forces or illness limit their resources of health, time, or money? We also see the THE HANGED MAN reversed in position 9, Issue That Needs to Be Resolved. This indicates that both partners' ability to trust one another is the issue most in need of resolution. Rachel will need to be sure to align her actions with her ideals of unconditional support through hardship. The prosperous, generous, and stable SIX OF PENTACLES in position 10, the Likely Outcome of the Current Situation, suggests that she will indeed offer and receive the support she values.

Seth's Heart in the Relationship comes up as the ACE OF CUPS. He is overflowing with love and joy, and senses limitless potential in his connection with Rachel.

The Foundation of the Relationship is the EIGHT OF WANDS: the feeling of adventure, productive activity, and communication that Seth and Rachel inspire in one another. They travel together, inspire one another's creative projects, and communicate readily.

The conflict of the FIVE OF SWORDS in the position of this couple's Already Established Ways of Relating shows us that Rachel and Seth have learned how to fight. A big disagreement a few months into their relationship allowed them the opportunity to learn how to face their fears and faults with the intention of pulling through together and growing stronger.

TEMPERANCE appears in position 5, the Couple's Conscious Goals. Both Seth and Rachel are artists. They value making art together and supporting one another to make art, as well as cultivating the artistic state of harmonious flow between them in their relationship. They find that they temper one another's extremes and intend to continue to do so, while also resisting the temptation to indulge in the other's minor addictions and extremes. The reversal indicates that the potential of this card is latent. Rachel and Seth have talked about creating a big project together, but they are unsure about the medium or subject of their collaboration. They might do well to look ahead to the card in position 9, representing the issues of trust that need to be resolved between them—their collaborative art project might be an excellent location to explore this issue and reach toward resolution.

THE WORLD in position 7 shows us that Seth sees himself in this relationship as celebrating their partnership as a culminating experience in his life. He feels complete with Rachel.

Rachel sees herself again as a Knight. This time, the KNIGHT OF PENTACLES in position 8. While Pages are beginners, students, young people, or apprentices, Knights represent the next stage of growing up, in which we have a strong idea of where we are going, yet still have more to learn. Rachel's idealism or naïveté about shared use of resources in partnership, as well as untested ideas about hardship and abundance, are emphasized by the Pentacles in this Knight card. We see that, as a knight rather than a page, Rachel is no longer a beginner in the way she loves, but she knows she has more learning to do before she becomes a Queen or King of Pentacles.

As mentioned earlier, the reversed Hanged Man in position 9, Issue That Needs to Be Resolved, points to trust issues. Seth and Rachel talk often about the importance of defending one another, as they are an interracial couple whose challenges vary from moment to moment depending on who they are interacting with. They decide to make a piece of art about their questions of trust. The Six of Pentacles in position 10, the Likely Outcome of the Current Situation, suggests that through doing so, they will at the very least resolve for now any issues around hardship and shared resources, arriving at prosperity, stability, and generosity.

COMPARING YOUR OPTIONS

The Comparing Your Options spread is great for decision-making because along with a breakdown of the main pros and cons of each option, it also shows us the issue at the heart of our considerations, offering a way to gauge which pros and cons are most important.

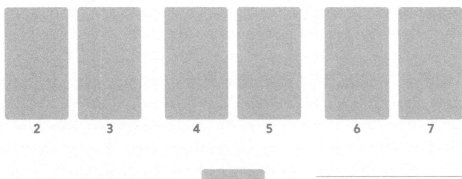

POSITION 1	Essential Consideration Underlying All Options
POSITION 2	Benefit of Option A
POSITION 3	Drawback of Option A
POSITION 4	Benefit of Option B
POSITION 5	Drawback of Option B
POSITION 6	Benefit of Option C
POSITION 7	Drawback of Option C

Sample Comparing Your Options Reading

Zak is in his mid-thirties and is unhappy in his job as a sign painter. He is a talented musician who has enjoyed a measure of success, but he has also experienced enough rejection that he is wondering whether he will ever have a career in music. Zak's options, as he sees them, are:

A Create his own record label and produce his own music.

B Focus all his efforts into getting picked up by a record label.

C Seek a job in tech that will offer him a stable income and the ability to make music as a hobby.

2

3

4

5

6

7

1

POSITION 1 The Tower

POSITION 2 The Moon, Reversed

POSITION 3 Four of Wands, Reversed

POSITION 4 Two of Swords

POSITION 5 Queen of Cups, Reversed

POSITION 6 Knight of Cups, Reversed

POSITION 7 The Chariot, Reversed

Essential Consideration Underlying All Options

THE TOWER, in position 1, the Essential Consideration Underlying All Options, tells Zak that he must break free from a current situation that is not working. Whichever option Zak chooses, he has to make a serious break away from his current sign painting job and from his current mentality of unhappiness and resentment.

Option A: Zak Creates His Own Record Label

What would be the benefit for Zak of producing his own music? THE MOON, reversed, offers a strange benefit: self-avoidance. The Moon, reversed, signifies remaining stuck in old emotional patterns. While avoiding the feelings of worthlessness that come up when he gets rejected by other record companies may be a superficial benefit for Zak, it does not comply with The Tower's insistence that Zak make a clean break from his current situation.

The FOUR OF WANDS, reversed, signals something very similar: anything Zak achieved under his own record label would not feel worthy of celebration to him. In his heart of hearts, he knows that striking out on his own allows him to remain an outsider who avoids facing the issues of rejection and conformity that he needs to explore in order to grow.

Option B: Zak Focuses His Energy and Resources on Getting Picked Up by a Record Label

The benefit of option B is represented by the TWO OF SWORDS. This card is not one of easy answers, but it does indicate intuitive answers. Choosing option B would force Zak to go within for answers to questions he has avoided for years. It is unclear whether this would mean a successful career, as the Two of Swords indicates uncertainty. However, the exploration it prompts could be powerful inspiration for Zak's next album.

The drawback of pursuing option B is represented by the QUEEN OF CUPS, reversed. This would be an emotionally draining experience, and Zak would likely have to deal with manipulative people and may even come to feel like a victim.

Option C: Zak Pursues a Different Career

The KNIGHT OF CUPS, reversed, represents the benefits of Zak funding his music practice through a lucrative career unrelated to music. This card shows Zak unable to express himself. It is a card of creative block, disappointment, and—Zak's recurring issue—fear of rejection. When Zak sees this card, he is unsure why this would be a benefit, and he wonders if the unconscious block that underlies his fear of rejection is actually more terrifying than he thought, to the extent that a life of creative block would almost seem to be a benefit. In the position of Drawbacks, THE CHARIOT, reversed, is yet another card of disappointment.

Conclusion

It appears that B is Zak's best option, but since it is still not very appealing, Zak decides to focus on changes he can make in the short term that could help him improve his outlook and create better future options. He decides to lay one more spread, the Triquetra Outcome Management spread (see next page) to improve his perspective.

TRIQUETRA OUTCOME MANAGEMENT

When things in your life feel bleak, or you have just done a reading in which the outcome card seemed discouraging, the Triquetra Outcome Management spread will reveal energies and qualities you can use to change your path. You'll likely find it helpful to not read reversals when using this spread, but rather go with the upright meaning of all three cards in this spread.

POSITION 1 Self, Individual Unconscious, Love

POSITION 2 Collective Unconscious, Responsibility, Contribution to the Whole, Honor

POSITION 3 Intuition, Higher Wisdom, Protection

Sample Triquetra Outcome Management Reading

Zak, whose options we got to know in the previous spread, follows his Comparing Your Options spread with a Triquetra Outcome Management spread to open his mind and help him persevere in seeking new options.

1

2

3

POSITION 1   Eight of Pentacles

POSITION 2   Seven of Pentacles

POSITION 3   Nine of Pentacles

All cards in this spread are in the suit of Pentacles, which emphasizes career and making money. The fact that these are three consecutive Pentacles cards indicates that one stage of effort will lead to the next, and it is more than likely that all this effort will ultimately culminate in a prosperous, comfortable, NINE OF PENTACLES lifestyle.

The EIGHT OF PENTACLES appears in position 1, Self, Individual Unconscious, Love. This affirms that Zak is a very industrious person. No matter what path he chooses, he will be able to put his nose to the grindstone and get the work done. He has a talent for breaking projects down into manageable tasks and accomplishing them. Considering the position of this card, Zak can consider his work on his music career an act of devotion—to himself and to his audience.

Position 2, Collective Unconscious, Responsibility, Contribution to the Whole, Honor, offers Zak the SEVEN OF PENTACLES, a card of pending success. The outcome may look uncertain now, but Zak has already invested so much time, effort, and resources in his music that as long as he carries through with his art, he will experience the rewards of his investment, multiplied. The music Zak makes tells stories of people whom history has tried to erase and offers nourishment to the collective imagination. Zak has a responsibility to continue pursuing his music career in the name of a much bigger collective purpose.

Zak's card in position 3, Intuition, Higher Wisdom, Protection, is the Nine of Pentacles. This indicates that Zak is guided by abundance and serenity. When Zak sees this card, the part of him that strives for a life of music and culture feels affirmed, and he knows he can believe in the pending success seen in the Seven of Pentacles. There is wisdom in striving for a life of beauty.

Can I Create My Own Tarot Spread?

Yes! I frequently create spreads on the spot, based on a client's unique questions and situation. Generally, you can lay a central card for the overall answer to a question, plus one card for each supporting factor you can identify beforehand.

The positioning of the cards can reflect the way in which you feel the factors relate to each other. For example, as we saw in the Past/Present/Future spread (page 36) and the Celtic Cross spread (page 45), chronology is often illustrated in a left (past) to right (future) fashion. Be creative with the way you visualize the factors of a spread to relate to each other.

Overall, a reliable method for creating your own spread is to utilize a structure you know well. Because I am well-versed in the structure of fiction, I offer my novelist clients a spread in which I lay a card for each plot point of the Hero's Journey. If you are a chef, you might consider creating a spread (for any area of life) which mimics the stages or layers of a particular recipe. If you are an activist, you might create a spread based of the stages of a particular type of action.

Whatever method you use to understand and engage in the world, use the cards as an expression or extension of that method.

GROWING FROM THE TAROT

I USE THE CARDS TO HELP MY CLIENTS unlock creative blocks, deepen their inspiration, and become more aware of issues and values that underlie their personal lives and creative work. Through our work together, they align their inner creative work with the small and large actions they take in their life, which helps them live with more integrity and finish their projects. My method often boils down to honoring challenges and blocks as windows into our rich, endlessly inspiring inner lives. I encourage you to use the cards for yourself in this manner.

When we honor our experience for what it is, rather than ignore it when it's not what we want or force it to become what it's not, we experience the relief of acceptance. We gain perspective. When we express our inner reality as it is—beautiful or ugly, manageable or overwhelming, new or familiar—we open up a realm of possibility.

From there, we have the choice to either obey our fears and other people's standards or to live in alignment with the reality we've imagined, the vision to which our intuition has led us.

The method I offer you in this chapter is this: simple meditation on the cards that come up to see what feelings, associations, and narratives arise. Then, we match the experiences that arose during meditation to the definitions of the cards. This act of naming elements of our inner experience often provides insight and epiphanies, which we can then further explore and express through art, conversation, or journaling. Gaining awareness of our experience in this way often illuminates or even shifts our paradigm, sparking change and growth in our lives. I believe it's important to continue our relationship with the cards that spark this growth, returning to them for guidance on how to integrate our insights into our actions to further empower ourselves and our communities.

The individual techniques in this chapter comprise my method for self-exploration and growth with the tarot. They can be used one after another in one sitting, over a period of days, weeks, or months. This method is applicable no matter the type of question you bring to the tarot. Your question could be about your career, family, health, romance, spirituality, or any other area of life. All the areas of life are fundamentally connected. When we believe ourselves to be working out an issue of love, for example, we will find that we also feel the effect of that question and growth in our work life. If we are to gain deep insight and truly grow from our practice of tarot, our reflection must happen on a profound level, where all the areas of our lives and all the aspects of ourselves are connected.

CONNECTING WITH OUR INTUITION

When we use the tarot for growth and empowerment, we start by connecting with our intuition. How can the cards be lenses that help reveal to us our inner lives?

Exercises for Illuminating Your Inner Experience and Intuition

Use the cards to illuminate elements of your inner experience and prompt meditative inquiry into your inner life. How do we activate this lens inward? Sit with what arises. Open to it, and embrace it. This gives us knowledge about our reality and connects us with our intuition.

This first step is noticing and illuminating our experience and connecting with our intuition. In this first step, we are not trying to change our experiences or ourselves, we simply accept our present reality.

ONE-CARD MEDITATION

Go to a quiet place where you know you will not be interrupted. Prepare your deck as described in chapter 2, then pull one card.

Take a moment to absorb the imagery of the card. Notice the figure(s), symbols, landscape, mood, colors, card name, and card number. If any memorized meanings of the card come to mind, allow them to come, though knowing the official meanings of the cards is not necessary at all.

Notice what stands out to you on first glance and what stands out when you take a second look.

Continue to enter or connect with the card. In *21 Ways to Read a Tarot Card*, Mary K. Greer suggests standing in the position of a figure in the card, closing your eyes, and finding out what you feel. You can also sit or stand in a comfortable, meditative position, close your eyes, and imagine the card in front of you. If you like, you can then imagine yourself entering the card and either becoming one of the figures or interacting with a figure, an object, or the environment of the card. You might also try a walking meditation with your eyes open to explore the environment depicted in the card with your imagination.

However you choose to envision or enter the card, give yourself time to become acquainted with the card and the associations it calls up in you. What memories, emotions, images, stories, questions, or changes in breathing, heart rate, or body temperature does this card evoke?

If nothing comes right away, simply describe the card to yourself, or ask yourself questions about the card, such as "What is happening in this card? Which season is depicted? Who does the figure seem to be?"

As clairvoyant tarot reader Alia Curtis told me and says in her workshops, "A lot of people want to go right into intuition. But the first things that come to mind are often thought, then intuition comes through." In other words, don't push yourself, but rather give yourself time to explore the card, your personal associations, and your intuition about how the card connects to your personal experience.

Finally, take a photo of the card you pulled, or otherwise make note of the card, so you can return to this card later for further guidance.

MEDITATION ON A SPREAD

Lay a spread from chapter 3 or one of your own invention.

Let your eyes drift over the cards and see what relationships you sense to be at play between the cards. Do the dynamics between the cards feel tense? Demanding? Supportive? Urgent? Unhurried? What are the relative ages of the figures in the cards? Are they facing toward or away from each other? What are the cards' similarities and differences?

Meditate on these relationships. What personal associations does this bring up?

Take a photo of the spread or otherwise note the cards and their positions, so you can return to this spread later for further guidance.

INTEGRATING INTUITION WITH CONSCIOUS AWARENESS

You likely noticed that in my suggestions for connecting with your intuition, I mentioned nothing about the official meanings of the cards. This is because, in many ways, the images can stand alone. Without words, they still carry conscious and subconscious meaning, but they are free of the mental constructs and emotional expectations that tend to accompany words and conscious thought. This freedom from conscious thought can help us make our initial connection with our intuition.

Now, however, this phase of the process is the time to bring your meditative, associative experience into conscious awareness. This means expressing your inner experience in the form of concepts by first using the lenses of the cards to help name your inner experience and spark insight, then to further explore that insight and integrate it into conscious awareness.

Tarot Card Definitions for Insight

Note how your associations and intuitive messages match up with the meanings of the cards. Recall or read the definition of the card or cards and see which parts of the definition(s) describe the experience you had while meditating. What does it feel like to name your experience? What does this help you express? What insights does this spark? Allow these archetypes, symbols, ideas, qualities, and themes to help you put words to the content of your intuition. You can take notes mentally or in a journal.

When we express our experience, we give form to the ineffable. Our vast, complex experience that we connected with through meditation now takes on the more defined shape of concepts. It takes practice to easefully connect our experience with the meanings of the cards, but when we do, we bring our unconscious mind and intuition into consciousness. We connect, briefly, our conscious and unconscious minds. This alignment of archetype and personal experience allows us a burst of insight and freedom in our lives. We get into the flow where everything in our life seems more interesting, meaningful, and carries more momentum.

Exploring and Integrating Insight through Creative Expression

The preceding exercise provides an initial spark of insight. After noting the connections between the tarot card meanings and your experience, further explore and integrate the resulting insight through any form of creative expression. Exploring and developing your initial insight in this way will help you integrate your insight into the conscious

way you regard your situation. When we want to increase our self-awareness and make positive changes in our lives, it's important to integrate the initial insight sparked by the cards into our consciousness and our daily actions.

Here are a few possible starting points:

- Craft a story, poem, song, choreography, or piece of visual art using one or more of the symbols or meanings in the tarot card(s).

- Redraw a card, with your own interpretation, symbols, or style.

- Write down one aspect of your experience that the tarot card(s) pointed you to. Would you like to honor this aspect? Or is it time to release this habit, belief, issue, or relationship dynamic? Create a ritual to express whatever it is, as well as to honor or release it.

- Write a dialogue between any three figures, objects, and/or landscapes in the cards.

Whatever form you choose, use your insight, the details of the situation about which you asked the tarot, or the tarot card itself to prompt your creative expression. This part of the process is exciting, but it's not always easy. Prepare to persevere through fear and dead ends. When we shape meaning, we go into the unknown.

While our intuition guides us—and the more you practice this, the more your intuition will guide you—we're still in a place of learning through trial and error. One way to think of this is that our intuition guides us through the darkness, leading us to the things we need to bump into in order to learn their contours and the dynamic of their placements relative to each other and to the rest of our life. Expression is an important part of integrating the insight gained in the associative realm into the conscious mind, as well.

Don't worry if any of these exercises take you away from your original idea or plan. That's what happens when we follow our intuition.

INTEGRATING INSIGHT WITH ACTION

Growth happens simply in expressing a truth. By expressing our experience—whether through art, conversation, journaling, or any other form of creative expression—we release old fears and beliefs, and uncover new ones. The way we speak and act changes slightly. We find ourselves more open, peaceful, adventurous, and able to love. The changes in our life can start happening rapidly when we're open to them.

Return to the original card or spread you have been working with. After experiencing the momentum of expression, it's time to channel that energy into deliberate action, growth, and empowerment.

Spend a moment meditating on the card(s). See what perspective you now have on the card

and on this aspect of your life. Feel the connection that has formed between this card and the aspect of your life you have been exploring. See the inner change that has already taken place since first pulling this card.

Reflect on your intuitive sense of the dynamics being portrayed in the card(s), as well as on your role therein. What do the cards tell you is the right response, action, or next step to take? Do the inspirations of the cards, as well as their warnings about their shadow sides (see page 39), suggest that you should:

- Persevere on your current path?
- Change course?
- Cooperate with others?
- Step into a leadership role?
- Ask for something you need?
- Define your boundaries?
- Make peace?
- Take the risk?
- Conserve your energy?
- Hold back until the situation becomes clearer?
- Extend compassion to yourself or someone else?

Your fears and habits might have some strong opinions about the course of action you "should" take. But what does your intuition tell you to do?

Positive Qualities

Every card has positive qualities. Regardless of whether you have been working with the card's shadow side or excessive quality, turn now to the card's positive qualities. Even if you have pulled the Ten of Swords, which shows a bleeding corpse stabbed by ten swords, you can focus on its metaphorical qualities of detox and release. If you have pulled a card of strife, such as the Five of Swords, consider how you can act to compassionately transform the situation.

Make a list of ways you could embody the card's positive qualities in specific situations and relationships in your life. Choose one or two to follow through on. If you need an extra boost of courage, pull another card to reveal an element of your life that supports you with this goal. Optionally, you might also pull a card for what might hinder you or draw your attention away from the matter at hand.

Ask for Guidance

Through meditation (see One-Card Meditation on page 64), envision yourself entering the card or spread. Ask a character therein for guidance regarding action. Allow the words or gift they offer you to intuitively come to you. Take note of the advice or gift you receive.

If the figure in the card does not represent you (or an aspect of yourself), but rather someone in your life—this can especially be the case with court cards—ask your intuition about the best ways to interact with that person, given the qualities you have explored, and/or pull another card to illuminate a helpful quality you can bring to the situation or to the relationship.

PART 2

THE CARDS

5

THE MAJOR ARCANA

THIS CHAPTER EXPLORES THE CARDS of the Major Arcana in detail. Cards 1 to 21 comprise the Fool's Journey in which The Fool, the adventure-seeker within each of us, travels through life's major experiences, represented in these 21 archetypal personas and experiences, to gain knowledge, grow, and achieve an epitome of freedom, joy, and love.

Each Major Arcana card description includes an interpretation of the card, upright and reversed, along with information about the symbols in its imagery, as well as its associated element, astrological sign/planetary association, and numerological significance.

I've chosen to use the gender-neutral pronoun "they" to describe most of the figures in the Major Arcana and later in the Minor Arcana. Most of the Minor Arcana cards depict men, though they are theoretically meant to apply to people of any gender. Many of the male and female figures of the court and Major Arcana are excessively gendered, in my opinion. I've noticed throughout my readings with clients that the clearly gendered cards of the court and Major Arcana (both masculine and feminine), though meant to represent elements within people of any gender, tend to hinder seekers from connecting to cards across genders. My use of the gender-neutral pronoun intends to help you make this leap to fully enter the cards, regardless of the gender or figure portrayed.

THE FOOL.

ALSO KNOWN AS The Jester

KEYWORDS Leap of Faith, Innocence, Adventure

ELEMENT Air

ASTROLOGY Uranus

NUMEROLOGY 0

The Fool is our sense of adventure, our inner child who sets out gleefully and impulsively to see the world and gain experience. The path of the Major Arcana is known as the Fool's Journey; each card represents a lesson or phase of life that The Fool experiences.

The Fool travels lightly on their journey, carrying all their belongings in just a small bundle. The Fool is hard to pin down. They are unknowable and endlessly playful. Just when we think we know something or have achieved anything, like a jester The Fool strips away pretentions and solid answers.

Pulling The Fool indicates taking risks and leaps of faith. The dog in this card symbolizes instinct and self-preservation, as well as social mores, which The Fool ignores. The dog tries to warn The Fool of the danger of stepping off the cliff, but The Fool ignores the little dog, because we must accept danger to go into the world.

Dreaming at the edges of cliffs and believing in only the best possibilities, the hopeful, idealistic Fool reminds us that it's never too late to follow our dreams. If you have pulled The Fool, enjoy your sense of play and optimism. Catch yourself before you do anything too foolhardy—but remember that confining yourself to convention is sometimes the silliest and most foolish thing a person can do.

Reversed

Reversed, The Fool indicates that you are being either too impulsive or not impulsive enough. If you have been going overboard in your adventures, it is time to rein it in before anyone gets hurt. On the other hand, if you haven't gone out dancing or had a good laugh in a while, do something fun.

Symbolism

CLIFF Leap of faith

DOG Instinct, self-preservation, social mores

WHITE ROSE Innocence

MOUNTAINS Challenges to overcome and accomplishments to reach

SUN Conscious awareness, light, energy, and guidance from a higher power

Mystic Meanings

The numerological significance of 0 points to infinite potential. The Fool has yet to become someone with an identity or role. Instead, The Fool's role is to reduce arrogance and insistence on rules down to zero.

Air is The Fool's element. The Fool is light on their feet, lighthearted, and idealistic—sometimes with their head in the clouds. Their sense of adventure propels them to scale great heights, ascending mountains up into the atmosphere.

Posing a Question

Why am I feeling bored in my relationship with my partner?

In response to a question of matters of the heart, The Fool points to our inner child. It is essential for your health in all areas of life to feed your creativity and your sense of adventure and fun. In what ways is your current relationship neglecting or silencing your inner child? What needs to change? Once these issues are clear to you, you'll be better able to state your needs and find a solution that will renew your relationship.

In astrology, The Fool is associated with Uranus, the planet of individuality, originality, and breaking tradition. Uranus's energy is androgynous, like The Fool's.

Supporting and Opposing Cards

The Fool is a card of endless beginnings. If an Ace or Aces from the Minor Arcana also appear in a reading, the message of a new beginning is emphasized.

The Hierophant and The Fool always butt heads. They are the archetypes of convention and irreverence. Both cards appearing in a reading signifies conflict between these two forces in one's life.

THE MAGICIAN.

ALSO KNOWN AS The Juggler

KEYWORDS Creativity, Manifestation, Ability

ELEMENT Quintessence

ASTROLOGY Mercury

NUMEROLOGY 1

The Magician makes things happen. The Magician always finds a way to manifest plans into reality. Their ability to envision what they wish to manifest, along with their conviction in manifesting it, gives them 360-degree vision, noticing opportunities and resources that others overlook or don't deem themselves worthy of pursuing.

The Magician is optimistic and willing to take an unconventional route to manifest their vision: They care more about putting an idea into action than they do about what others may think of them along the way. If you have pulled The Magician for yourself, you are creative, flexible, and adaptive. You have strong concentration and the willpower to actualize your plans and goals.

Reversed

Reversed, The Magician's power is either latent or being used without integrity. Watch out for someone who may be charming you in order to take advantage of you. Make sure you are only completing projects that have strong integrity and that your means of achieving your goals live up to the intended integrity of your project.

Alternately, if you are feeling stuck and powerless, focus on the vision you want to achieve. You may be stuck because you are only considering conventional routes. What alternate routes or resources are available to you? Striking out on your own to achieve your goals, rather than allowing yourself to remain stuck because a path isn't being offered to you by someone else, will be worth the bouts of momentary confusion.

Symbolism

LEMNISCATE (SIDEWAYS FIGURE 8) Infinity

VERTICAL BATON Interconnection of matter, consciousness, and the divine; "As Above, So Below"

PENTACLE, SWORD, CUP, WAND Four elements, four Minor Arcana suits, the range of resources available to The Magician and spheres of influence

YELLOW Consciousness and manifestation

OUROBOROS (SNAKE SWALLOWING ITS TAIL) Wholeness, infinity

ROSES Passion, beauty, creativity

LILIES Purity, integrity

Mystic Meanings

The numerological significance of the number 1 is unity and power. The Magician has incredible power to manifest and create, in large part because The Magician does not see themself as separate from the rest of the universe. They tap into all available resources and inspiration to put plans into action.

The Magician's element is actually ether, or quintessence, the alchemical denotation of the divine spirit that fills all four natural elements with life.

Mercury is The Magician's astrological counterpart. Like The Magician, Mercury is the planet that helps everyday logistics, transportation, technology, and communication go smoothly.

Posing a Question

I'm considering a career change. What will guide me in making this switch?

Pulling The Magician suggests that you are indeed embarking on a new beginning. New and positive career opportunities are coming to you. Choose between them with confidence—do not allow your vision to be limited by anyone or by your own self-doubt. The Magician urges you to have confidence in your vision for your new career and for your contribution to society. Weigh your job, internship, or education options according to how they will best support you to achieve this vision, not according to how prestigious or well-trodden certain paths may be. The right path for you might be an original one.

Supporting and Opposing Cards

The Chariot shares The Magician's concentration and clarity of purpose. Aces reinforce The Magician's meaning of opportunities and beginnings.

In opposition to The Magician, The Devil constrains our vision and narrows our possibilities. Minor Arcana cards of blockage or pause, such as the Two of Swords, inhibit The Magician's energy, but to a lesser degree than does The Devil.

THE HIGH PRIESTESS.

ALSO KNOWN AS The Female Pope

KEYWORDS Inner Knowledge, Intuition, Duality

ELEMENT Water

ASTROLOGY Moon

NUMEROLOGY 2

The High Priestess sits before a veil that divides the seen world from the unseen realms of feeling and spirituality. They are the gatekeeper of the knowledge that lies beyond the veil. They quietly and intuitively sense who to lead out of their daily reality into a deeper spiritual experience.

Pulling The High Priestess indicates that you, or an important figure in your life, are deeply intuitive, even psychic. The High Priestess is a spiritual teacher (regardless of whether or not this is their title) who offers profound wisdom beyond the illusions of this life to those who are willing to open their eyes.

A mystery is at hand. Something is hidden. You must solve this one by going inward. Then, like Persephone from Greek mythology returning to the land of the living, you must forge a bridge between your inner and outer life so that you can live in integrity with more serious truths.

Since The High Priestess's alternate name, The Female Pope, does not denote an actual position within Catholicism, this card is suggestive of religious figures who do not conform to dominant or patriarchal religious structures. This card values spiritual ways of knowing that are private, personal, and possibly secret or hidden.

Reversed

Reversed, The High Priestess suggests secrets or secrecy. You may be keeping a secret in order to deceive someone, or someone is hiding something from you. You may be ignoring or denying your spirituality. Your intuition and premonition skills are latent, but you are brushing them off. Allow them to come to the foreground.

Symbolism

CRESCENT MOON, WATERY GOWN Intuition

CROWN Waxing, waning, and full moon; maiden, mother, and crone; Isis, goddess of wisdom, magic, and restorer of souls

PILLARS Solomon's Temple; the B and J stand for the pillars' names, *Boaz* and *Jachin*, which combined mean, "In him it is Strength, He shall establish."

BLUE Clarity of consciousness

TORA The Torah

POMEGRANATE SEEDS Persephone, who lived half the time above and half below ground

Mystic Meanings

In numerology, the number 2 carries the meanings of duality and balance. The High Priestess creates balance between her inner and outer life. Though the number 2 represents partnership, The High Priestess emphasizes our relationship with ourselves and our relationship with the divine. The High Priestess values privacy and solitude. Twos also represent choice. The High Priestess insists that we trust our gut when making a decision.

The High Priestess is associated with the moon and with the element of water. The moon connects us to our subconscious, intuition, and emotions. It attunes us to our inner fluctuations,

> ### Posing a Question
>
> *What is important for me to know about my romantic life at this time?*
>
> When you pull The High Priestess in response to a relationship question, the cards are telling you to focus on your connection with yourself and your spirituality. To do this, you need some degree of solitude. This solitude or separation doesn't have to be drastic, but The High Priestess does insist that, right now you prioritize nurturing your inner world over your romantic life.

questions, and transformations. Our inner knowing is fluid and constantly changing. Like water, our intuition flows anywhere, taking whatever form it needs to, easily shifting and adapting amidst change. These facets of The High Priestess remind us to trust our inner knowing, even and especially inner knowing that precedes thought or subverts reason.

Supporting and Opposing Cards

The Two of Swords supports The High Priestess's inward focus, intuition, and patience. The Moon is another card of intuition, though The Moon's focus is on instinct, while The High Priestess emphasizes calm inner knowledge.

Cards that represent entirely outward action and rational thought, such as the Knight of Swords, oppose The High Priestess.

III

THE EMPRESS.

ALSO KNOWN AS The Mother

KEYWORDS Beauty, Motherhood, Creativity

ELEMENT Earth

ASTROLOGY Venus

NUMEROLOGY 3

The Empress is the creative state, embodied. She, he, or they are a mother, endlessly creative and absorbed in love and the sensuality of creativity. Inspiration knows no bounds. The Empress surpasses ordinary boundaries in many spheres of life. As a mother, pregnant with ideas or a child, they create through love. They nurture their children, relationships, ideas, and projects, and help all people in their life grow.

If you have pulled this card for yourself, you cherish your emotions as ways of knowing the world and connecting with yourself. You are connected to your body, and you luxuriate in sensual and aesthetic pleasure. The Empress's aesthetic sense is embodied in their comfortable throne marked with the symbol of Venus.

When The Empress becomes exaggerated or imbalanced, they care for others but neglect themself, they are overprotective or overindulgent with their children, or they use their role as mother to define their identity or to manipulate others.

Reversed

Reversed, The Empress indicates difficulty with motherhood. This might come about as infertility, being forced into motherhood, dealing with a stifling definition of motherhood or expectation to be nurturing, or difficulties in your relationship with your mother or mother figure.

The reversed Empress can also suggest a negative relationship with your body and sense of pleasure. The Empress, reversed, indicates you may be feeling a lack of abundance and struggling with creative blocks that result from denying your relationship with beauty, pleasure, art, and your inner child. Take some time to address this.

Symbolism

STARRY CROWN Creativity, motherhood, unity

LAUREL WREATH CROWN Success, power

POMEGRANATE SEEDS ON ROBE Fertility, rebirth; Persephone, who lived half the time above and half below ground

SYMBOL OF VENUS Femininity, beauty, love

WHEAT Fertility and abundance

SCEPTER Sovereignty

WATERFALL Fluidity

FOREST The unconscious

SCEPTER WITH GLOBE Sovereignty, earthly realm, ability to co-create with a partner

Mystic Meanings

In numerology, 3 is the number of synthesis and creativity: two things coming together to create a third, as two parents conceive a child or a comparison of two things creates a third element of metaphor. The dynamic balance of these three-part relationships concerns The Empress.

This archetype is embodied by the element of earth. The Empress, the mother, grounds us. She supports us and helps us know our roots.

Posing a Question

I just started a neighborhood community group. How can I best serve these gatherings?

Pulling The Empress in answer to this question affirms your talent for fostering connection among people, leading others, encouraging the group's vision and growth, and bringing your natural sense of beauty, creativity, abundance, and joy to the group. These qualities are needed and valued in your community. Continuing to be a good leader will best serve the group.

Venus, the planet of beauty and love, is associated with The Empress. The Empress finds, creates, and offers grounding through beauty and relationships.

Supporting and Opposing Cards

Cards of abundance, such as the Ten of Pentacles, emphasize The Empress's boundless creativity, fertility, and abundance.

The generous, nurturing Empress conflicts with the miserly, fearful Four of Pentacles. However, cards of mature discipline and stability, such as The Emperor, complement the flowing Empress.

THE EMPEROR.

ALSO KNOWN AS The Grandfather

KEYWORDS Reliability, Fatherhood, Responsibility

ELEMENT Fire

ASTROLOGY Aries

NUMEROLOGY 4

The Emperor is your most reliable family member, friend, or community leader. They are the person you can always count on to take responsibility for getting things done, who will follow through on their word. While The Emperor's counterpart, The Empress, overflows with creative ideas and nurtures possibility, The Emperor deems which ideas are most viable and effective, and carries them out. The Emperor plans, delegates, structures, and carries out projects. While The Empress helps us experience timelessness and cultivate love and beauty, The Emperor helps us operate within a strict schedule and produce finite outcomes.

The arid canyon pictured in this card, with just a small river running through it, indicates that too much emphasis on order and structure alone can suck us dry. At their worst, The Emperor is a destructive, power-hungry, authoritarian leader. However, when we have a meaningful project to complete, and we work toward the common good, The Emperor gives us the discipline and wherewithal to achieve great things and provide support to many people.

If you have pulled The Emperor for yourself, you are in a position of authority or responsibility. Through self-discipline and reason, you are achieving ambitious aims that affect many people. Important decisions, final decisions, and last-minute decisions all fall on you. Pulling The Emperor can also indicate that you are working out questions relating to authority, systems, and power.

Reversed

When The Emperor, reversed, reveals that the upright qualities of this card are latent in you or in your situation, it is time to become more assertive, decisive, and attentive to schedules, materials, and productivity. Alternately, the reversed Emperor can indicate a coup, revolution, or overthrowing of leadership. This might be a celebratory event, or it might feel like sabotage or indicate an undermining force in your life.

Symbolism

ANKH SCEPTER Authority, life

ARMOR AND BURGUNDY ROBES Warrior king

GOLDEN SPHERE Globe, dominion, territory

RAMS Aries, energetic, competitive

ARID CANYON Harsh conditions, harsh rule

Mystic Meanings

The numerological meaning of the number 4 is material achievement, structure, and order.

As we see from the rams' heads on The Emperor's throne, this archetype is associated with Aries—an active, rationally minded, ambitious doer.

Associated with the element of fire, The Emperor has charisma and energy. This active, outer-world energy can either drive big ambitions, thereby sustaining big projects and productions, or this fire energy can cause destruction.

Posing a Question

What do I need to be aware of in my leadership approach?

When you ask the cards about your responsibilities, authority, or leadership skills and receive The Emperor, you are encouraged to look into the areas in which more structure or accountability is necessary. Be discerning about what structure you can and should provide, and in what areas, ways, or situations you should allow your children, students, employees, or team members more room for discovery, exploration, relaxation, play, creativity, emotional health, interpersonal growth, and unconditional love. Reflect, also, on your own relationship to authority, possibly going all the way back to your relationship with your father or with a masculine parent figure.

Supporting and Opposing Cards

The Justice card reinforces The Emperor's values of reason and logic. The Hierophant shares with The Emperor an emphasis on structure.

Although The Empress is considered an opposing card, The Empress's opposite qualities of creativity and new life complement The Emperor's stability and discipline. Appearing together, they often indicate an influential couple.

THE HIEROPHANT.

ALSO KNOWN AS Pope, Teacher, Saturn

KEYWORDS Education, Knowledge, Religion, Conformity

ELEMENT Earth

ASTROLOGY Taurus

NUMEROLOGY 5

The Hierophant interprets, protects, and teaches sacred mysteries. The keys at their feet indicate that they hold the keys to unlocking wisdom, spiritual truths, or the kingdom of heaven. These keys have been codified within institutions of tradition, spirituality, and knowledge or any organization or community formed to preserve, develop, and share knowledge.

In the Rider-Waite-Smith deck, The Hierophant is depicted as a pope, but can be any benevolent and compassionate spiritual or intellectual leader. In ancient Greece, a hierophant was anyone who introduced others to holiness. If you have pulled The Hierophant for yourself, you are someone who serves as a moral compass for others. Your intellect, tradition, and knowledge allow you to bridge heaven and earth, reminding everyone in your life of the unity of divinity and earth, the unity of our souls and bodies.

As a bridge between spiritual and material worlds, The Hierophant offers blessings and sacraments, such as marriage and last rites, and generally communicates the divine to their students and followers.

Reversed

Reversed, The Hierophant can reveal criticism, poor leadership, bad advice, and being misled by an egotistical authority figure. On the other hand, The Hierophant, reversed, can represent a free-spirited visionary, giving you permission to forge your own path.

Symbolism

RED ROBES Earth, as well as energy and action in the material world

GOLD SCEPTER Heaven, three crosses (holy trinity)

TRIPLE CROWN Holy trinity

HAND GESTURE Blessing

RED ROSES Love

WHITE LILIES Purity

PILLARS Law and liberty

Mystic Meanings

In numerology, the number 5 represents healing, as well as the link between spirit and humankind. The Hierophant's Greek mythological association is the centaur Chiron, referred to as the wounded healer.

Associated with Taurus, an earth sign, The Hierophant offers us spiritual grounding. Just as a Taurus promotes harmony but can be stubborn in their methods, The Hierophant insists that conformity to tradition is the ticket to harmony.

Supporting and Opposing Cards

If both The Emperor and The Hierophant appear in a reading, structure is an important issue or theme. Combined with the Four of Wands, The Hierophant indicates marriage or the completion of a period of spiritual or educational training.

The free spirits, The Hanged Man and The Fool, often indicate conflict with The Hierophant's institution.

Posing a Question

I am at a crossroads. What do I need to be aware of to make my next move?

Pulling The Hierophant in answer to this question suggests going to an academic, religious, or professional mentor or to an institution of teaching and learning for growth, development, and answers. Rather than relying on speculation or pure intuition, it's time to learn facts and skills and become versed in a tradition. Stay aware of your relationship to conformity, but overall, seek and offer mentorship through a spiritual tradition or academic institution. Right now, a conventional path will get you where you need to go.

THE LOVERS.

The Lovers indicate a time of life-changing connection and love. Not limited to erotic or romantic love, this card encompasses the experience of merging with a larger consciousness through ideas, spirituality, or interpersonal love.

To reach such heights of meaning and depths of love, we have to make choices about where we invest our devotion—otherwise, we get trapped on the surface, scattered amongst our options, feeling indecisive and unfulfilled.

If you have pulled The Lovers, you know that you have made or are about to make a commitment that allows you to reach a deeper level of experience. The object of your commitment and desire can range from a person, job, or role in your community to a project of art or thought. Whatever or whomever you commit to, your merging will lead you to a higher consciousness and a feeling of spiritual connection with all beings.

ALSO KNOWN AS Love, Marriage

KEYWORDS Connection, Fulfillment, Love, Choice

ELEMENT Air

ASTROLOGY Gemini

NUMEROLOGY 6

Reversed

Reversed, The Lovers indicate that a partnership or a creative, moral, or intellectual passion is not being honored. You or your partner is tempted by other influences. Whereas The Lovers, upright, indicates the importance of making decisions that honor depth of love, The Lovers, reversed, indicates uncertainty, confusion, disrespect, or betrayal. Be sure to honor the spirit of love in action and intention, whatever this may mean for you, and not just in appearance. Now is a time to take a deep breath and grow beyond past circumstances or temptations.

Symbolism

ADAM AND EVE Primeval partnership

ARCHANGEL RAPHAEL Higher consciousness, healing, love

MOUNTAIN Aspirations attainable through love

SUN Joy

Mystic Meanings

In numerology, 6 is the number of harmony, integration, and passivity. The Lovers indicates intimate harmony and integration with another person, cause, ideas, or beliefs. We are humbled by this experience, and we become "passive" in the sense that we get out of our own way to openly receive the gifts of love.

The Lovers are associated with the element of air. Love (whether for a person, a cause, a project, or something else) gives us access to a higher, collective consciousness. This is the air element: elevating and transcendent.

In astrology, The Lovers are associated with Gemini, twins who comprise one person and embody duality. Geminis show us that oneness is multifaceted and that unity and love are possible through joining difference. Additionally, choice and decisions are often concerns for Geminis, individuals who must make decisions for the benefit of both sides of themselves, the way that in relationship and partnership we must make decisions with the best interest of the whole at heart.

Posing a Question

I feel as if I need to take the day off from work. What's the likely consequence if I do?

If you receive The Lovers when asking about the consequences of an option you are considering, you can expect that choosing that option will bring you connection, inspiration, and a feeling of love. It might also suggest that this option will eventually present you with more options and possible temptations to choose from. In this case, taking the day off work will likely bring a day of fulfillment—just watch your relationship to temptation!

Supporting and Opposing Cards

In combination with The Lovers, The Hierophant offers a message supportive of marriage and commitment. The Two of Cups with The Lovers supports connection, love, and mutual fulfillment.

The solitude of The Hermit can mitigate the bond reflected by The Lovers.

THE CHARIOT.

ALSO KNOWN AS Victory, Triumphal Car

KEYWORDS Momentum, Breakthrough, Travel

ELEMENT Water

ASTROLOGY Cancer

NUMEROLOGY 7

Pulling things together is a major theme of The Chariot. This card features symbols from preceding cards in the Major Arcana. The wings on the chariot signify The Lovers' passion and higher purpose, the charioteer's wand reminds us of The Magician's power to manifest, the starry crown and canopy evoke the creativity of The Empress, the stone chariot mimics the throne of the sharp-minded, decisive Emperor, and the crescent shoulder plates mirror The High Priestess and her intuition.

If you have pulled The Chariot for yourself, you have the presence of mind to arrange all the elements of your life to run smoothly together, balancing opposing pieces of your life to give you momentum. Though you may have experienced a breaking point recently, things are now coming together. The dark and light sphinxes on this card signify opposites and the way you are able to reconcile these to unleash teamwork. The rush of excitement fuels your days.

Reversed

The Chariot's swift and directed momentum is either thwarted or spirals out of control when reversed. Addiction, indulgence, or egotism replace spirituality, and the path becomes filled with disappointments. Although The Chariot's upright qualities are latent at this time, they are present as potential. Ask for help to get yourself on a healthy and creative path, and convince yourself to take the reins of your life.

Symbolism

DARK AND LIGHT SPHINXES Reconciliation of "opposites," push and pull, balance; their positioning mirrors the symmetry in The Hierophant, suggesting meaningful structure

WAND The Magician, manifestation

CRESCENT MOONS The High Priestess, intuition

STARS The Empress, creativity, beauty

THRONE-LIKE STONE CHARIOT The Emperor, analytical thinking and leadership

WINGS The Lovers, love, moral choices, and higher consciousness

LAUREL WREATH Victory, power

Mystic Meanings

The numerological meaning of the number 7 is spirituality and tests. The Chariot's momentum is both intuitive and preconceived: You are filled with and driven by a spiritual purpose, *and* you cleverly navigate the tests and challenges that crop up along your way. Your spiritual momentum at this time may actually be coming from the tests you have endured.

The Chariot's element is water. The Chariot is all about flow. Sometimes it can carry the feeling of a dam breaking open, of pent-up energy finally being released and channeled into more exciting, adventurous, creative use. When you pull The Chariot, your life is a river with a swift current.

Astrologically, The Chariot is associated with the zodiac sign Cancer. Like their symbol the crab, Cancers are sensitive inside and protect themselves with a tough shell. The Charioteer's shell is their intellect, while much of their inner experience is emotional, intuitive, and spiritual.

Supporting and Opposing Cards

The Chariot's victory is emphasized by success cards, such as the Ace of Swords and The World.

Cards that indicate a pause oppose The Chariot, including the Two of Swords, The Four of Cups, and The Hanged Man.

Posing a Question

What should I keep in mind while I search for a new home?

If you receive The Chariot in answer to a question about settling down, you may want to hold off making a firm decision right now. This is likely a time of travel, breakthroughs, and motion for you, so considerations about settling down might be best saved for later. However, if you're convinced that now is the time to search for a home, make sure your home, like one of The Chariot's sphinxes, balances an opposite element of your life. Look for a home that will serve as a peaceful, stable counterpoint to your life's adventures. Your home should be in a location that does not hinder your access to your outer-world life.

ALSO KNOWN AS Lust, Fortitude

KEYWORDS Compassion, Perseverance, Power

ELEMENT Fire

ASTROLOGY Leo

NUMEROLOGY 8

Strength depicts a maiden taming a lion through compassion. By treating the lion with kindness and gentleness, the lion understands that he is safe and loved. His aggression melts away, and when the maiden places her hand near his mouth, he doesn't bite. The Strength card indicates any situation in which we achieve great things, earning respect and power, through kindness and love.

The Strength card represents a vision that is so strong, others can easily understand its purpose and willingly join in. The maiden has a vision of harmony, which she invites the lion into. If you have pulled the Strength card, your vision may be a business, a family, a community initiative, or any creative project. This card assures you that your vision is possible to achieve and worth the effort of doing so. It will have a profound effect in the lives of many people.

The lemniscate, the sideways figure eight hovering above the maiden's head, symbolizes eternity. Its ceaselessness gestures to the perseverance involved in sustaining a vision, and negotiating with others to become part of the vision and create a new reality.

In addition to emotional and mental strength, this card represents physical strength and vitality. However, as the maiden's kindness calms the ferocity of the lion, Strength suggests a disciplining and channeling of urges and impulses. We cannot get rid of our animal impulses and needs—the lion still must kill to eat; food, sex, and power are desires that will not go away—however, Strength shows us how to use our vitality for the common good, as much as this is possible.

Reversed

Reversed, Strength signals that you are being either too forceful or too passive in response to conflict. Channel the upright qualities of this card, compassion and gentle confidence, rather than adding to the violence of the situation or letting violence be carried out against you.

Symbolism

LION Power, courage, danger, leadership

LEMNISCATE (SIDEWAYS FIGURE 8) Infinity

RED ROSES Passion, love

MOUNTAIN Aspirations

YELLOW BACKGROUND Consciousness, vitality, and manifestation

Mystic Meanings

In numerology, the number 8 represents navigation, prosperity, and authority. Strength represents success, power, and compassionately navigating social (and internal) dynamics.

The element of fire is associated with this card; it illuminates Strength's passion, persistence, and confidence.

Strength's astrological link is the zodiac sign Leo, the lion. Leos are firm in their beliefs and they love hard—passionately, loyally, and protectively.

Posing a Question

The team leader of my project isn't open to my ideas. How can I get through to them?

In general, the Strength card emphasizes strength of vision. If you pull this card in answer to this question, think about the outcome you would like. Spend a little time getting clear about your vision. Tap into your confidence that the outcome you have in mind would benefit everyone involved. Set a meeting with the team leader to discuss the issue at hand. Start by finding common ground, the way the figure in the Strength card acknowledges the lion with kindness, and negotiate from there, staying true to your vision.

Supporting and Opposing Cards

Temperance reinforces Strength's balance. Combined with the Ten of Wands, Strength emphasizes a big vision or task that will require much physical and emotional strength to accomplish.

Cards in which our subconscious impulses overrun our consciousness, as in The Moon, or in which physical urges overturn our discipline, as in The Devil, combat the balance and discipline of Strength.

THE HERMIT.

ALSO KNOWN AS The Elder, Time

KEYWORDS Wisdom, Seeker, Inner Voice

ELEMENT Earth

ASTROLOGY Virgo

NUMEROLOGY 9

The Hermit is an elder who embodies wisdom and discretion. Their age gives them distance from the bustling world. The lamp they carry represents their inner voice, which they honor and explore. Regardless of your age, if you have pulled The Hermit for yourself, you are an old soul and a seeker of inner healing, wisdom, and truth.

You are on a pilgrimage to find your inner voice or spiritual truths. What questions have you been asking, and who or what are you seeking out in search of answers? Your pilgrimage might be a religious or spiritual one, or it might simply be about finding ways to make your daily life more meaningful, such as setting aside more time for daily walks or meditations, so you can hear yourself think.

How you spend your time is one of The Hermit's concerns. What are the most meaningful activities in your life right now? Spending enough time by ourselves is important for us to hear the guidance of our inner wisdom and our divine inner voice. However, pulling The Hermit does not necessarily indicate spending most of your time alone, but rather that you spend your time doing meaningful things with people you resonate with. Teachers may be particularly important right now. Overall, you are able to prioritize your inner or spiritual life.

Reversed

The Hermit, reversed, signifies that you might be too adamant about securing your alone time, setting your schedule, and giving off the appearance of pursuing a spiritual practice. What can you let go of, instead, to create more room to experience awe?

Alternately, you may be ignoring the wisdom your inner voice or a wise person in your life has been trying to share. You have the potential to gain much wisdom in your life right now, but only if you actively seek out a path of learning and reflection.

Symbolism

LANTERN Inner voice

DOWNWARD GAZE Retreat

STAFF Self-reliance

SIX-POINTED STAR Unity of heaven and earth

Mystic Meanings

In numerology, the number 9 represents completion and achievement of goals. As an elder or an old soul, The Hermit feels a sense of completion and achievement in their life. Nine is also a number of meditation, an important practice of The Hermit.

The Hermit's spiritual search is not idealistic, emotional, or socially active. Rather, it is grounded. The element of earth indicates that The Hermit takes their time to make their journey and uses material resources respectfully.

The Hermit is associated with the zodiac sign Virgo. Like The Hermit, Virgos have a gentle attunement to awe and wonder.

Posing a Question

What can I do to engage my disinterested students?

The Hermit emphasizes meaningful endeavors. They value exploring their inner world and seeking wisdom over superficial pastimes and busywork. The Hermit suggests your students need to find the material more meaningful and personally relevant. Find ways to help them connect personally to their studies so they can embody the spirit of The Hermit's pursuit of meaning.

Additionally, you might be in a time of seeking and questioning your own path and teaching methods. Bring curiosity and faith to your own path and to the classroom. Also seek the help of a mentor to guide you through your situation.

Supporting and Opposing Cards

Cards of meditation and reflection, such as The High Priestess and the Four of Swords, emphasize The Hermit's spiritual practice of inward exploration. The Hermit is compatible with The Hierophant as a teacher.

Cards of celebration, such as the Nine of Cups and the Four of Wands, hinder The Hermit's solitary peacefulness.

WHEEL of FORTUNE.

The Wheel of Fortune represents seasons and changes of fate. We spend our lives cycling through bouts of good and bad luck, times of joy and times of grief. We can learn to respond compassionately to turns for the worse and take responsibility for our actions in all situations, but oftentimes, we really cannot control what circumstances befall us.

The Wheel of Fortune likely indicates an unexpected change of fate. The Wheel of Fortune reminds us that nothing stays stable for long, but that history and patterns do repeat themselves and what goes around comes around.

You may be coming to recognize and understand your own patterns as well as those of the people and world around you. You are gaining both agency and acceptance, or equanimity. You are becoming more able to recognize what is yours to change and what issues you ultimately must leave up to fate or to the divine.

Reversed

The reversed Wheel of Fortune indicates that things have come to a standstill or, perhaps, closure. Be aware of whether you are trying to resist fate. Anything you try to avoid will inevitably come back to haunt you. Consider the immediate and long-term effects of your actions.

Symbolism

HEBREW LETTERS YHWH The unspeakable name of God

ALSO KNOWN AS Fate, The Wheel

KEYWORDS Change, Patterns, Fortune

ELEMENT Fire

ASTROLOGY Jupiter

NUMEROLOGY 10, Reduces to 1

TORA (LETTERS READ COUNTERCLOCKWISE) Torah

TARO (LETTERS READ CLOCKWISE) Tarot

ROTA (LETTERS READ CLOCKWISE FROM THE BOTTOM) Latin for *wheel*

ALCHEMICAL SYMBOLS Mercury, sulfur, water, salt

RED JACKAL-HUMAN Anubis, Egyptian god of the afterlife

SNAKE Wisdom, temptation

SPHINX Fateful riddles

ANGEL, EAGLE, LION, BULL Fixed signs of the zodiac (Aquarius, Scorpio, Leo, Taurus), four elements (air, water, fire, earth), four directions (north, south, east, west), four phases of life (infancy, youth, adulthood, old age)

Mystic Meanings

In numerology, the number 10 indicates both growth and repetition. When the digits are added together, the number 10 reduces to 1, the number of unity, beginnings, and power, and points to The Magician's volition and all-encompassing perspective.

The Wheel of Fortune is always turning. It is the crucible in which pieces of ourselves and our lives are destroyed and created anew.

The Wheel of Fortune's astrological association, Jupiter, reinforces this card's meanings of money and fortune, as Jupiter is the planet of abundance and expansion.

Posing a Question

My life feels like it's falling apart. How can I pull it back together?

In response to this question, the Wheel of Fortune advises you to focus on the patterns you know to be true in yourself and in your life. These patterns help you know the actions you can take, which will most likely take hold. This is not the time for wishful thinking, but rather for acting on what you know to be true through experience. Pay attention to cause and effect. This is a growing-up moment. You have an incredible opportunity to break a cycle. You can do this by taking responsibility for your own perspective and for the way you respond to change. Every situation is impermanent, including times of chaos or loss. .

Supporting and Opposing Cards

The Wheel of Fortune's meaning of breaking a cycle is reinforced by The Chariot (the breakthrough card) and, to a lesser extent, the Seven of each suit of the Minor Arcana.

Death or The Tower combined with the Wheel of Fortune emphasize the meaning of unexpected, fateful change.

Cards of stagnation appearing with the Wheel of Fortune indicate a resistance to change. The Four of Pentacles and the Four of Cups are two such cards.

JUSTICE.

ALSO KNOWN AS Adjustment

KEYWORDS Balance, Objectivity, Fairness, Equity

ELEMENT Air

ASTROLOGY Libra

NUMEROLOGY 11, Reduces to 2

Justice describes fairness, equity, and balance being restored to the extent that this is possible. In this card, the figure weighs the situation's various considerations (represented by the scales) and uses a clear, rational, objective mind (represented by their sword) to choose the correct course of action.

Part of Justice's balancing act involves balancing out their personal opinions and biases with objective awareness. Justice also maintains the ability to respond to the moral and practical demands of the situation at hand, while remaining true to ourselves. The curtain behind Justice gestures toward the realms of cosmic justice that govern karma, the law of cause and effect, better than humans can, but whose laws we aim to channel in our own dealings with justice.

Justice is also a card of making adjustments, specifically the adjustments that happen in moving from the abstract to the specific. Enacting fairness and creating balance and equality requires adjusting our understanding of rules, laws, and moral codes to assess the specifics of a particular situation. Following the Wheel of Fortune, Justice also describes the adjustments we must make in our lives following a change of fate. If you have pulled the Justice card, you are likely making decisions that restore balance to a disrupted life or an unfair situation.

Reversed

Reversed, Justice indicates undue feelings of injustice. Even though things haven't turned out in your favor, the outcome of this situation is actually best and most fair for everyone involved. At an extreme, this lack of perspective manifests as so many forms of prejudice, bias, and injustice. Corruption, opportunism, injustice, racism, xenophobia, sexism, ableism, transphobia, misogyny, heterosexism, and homophobia are just a few examples.

Symbolism

SCALES Weighing the factors of a decision

SWORD Rational thinking, objectivity

CURTAIN Veil beyond which lies the realm of cosmic justice

PILLARS Balance, support, legal institutions

Mystic Meanings

In numerology, 11 is a sacred number of spiritual insight. When the digits are added together, the number 11 reduces to 2, the number of duality, balance, fairness, choice, and partnership.

Associated with the element of air, Justice is rational. There is a feeling of weightlessness to Justice's objectivity.

Justice's astrological link to Libra, the scales, resonates with Libra values of balance and fairness.

Posing a Question

What is the deeper issue beneath the argument I had with my partner?

If you have pulled Justice, you and your partner likely experienced a major life change in the recent past, and you are both making adjustments. Be fair with each other and communicate frequently about what you each are going through. To reestablish equilibrium between you, make your adjustments day by day, check your assumptions about your partner's actions, and move forward in ways that promote fairness and equality between you. As Justice represents balance and reason, it is especially important at this time for you each to know your own needs and to take care of yourselves, as well as one another.

Supporting and Opposing Cards

Like Justice, The Emperor is concerned with rational order and real-world duty. Cards of outer-world balance, like the Two of Pentacles, and rational-minded fairness, such as the Queen of Swords, also support Justice.

Cards of oppression, such as The Devil or the Ten of Swords, or competition, such as the Five of Swords, oppose Justice.

THE HANGED MAN.

ALSO KNOWN AS
The Hanging Man

KEYWORDS Trust,
Self-Sacrifice, Waiting

ELEMENT Water

ASTROLOGY Neptune

NUMEROLOGY 12, Reduces to 3

The Hanged Man embodies trust in the universe. If you have pulled The Hanged Man, your trust and faith are being tested. Your life feels like it is in suspense. You are having trouble moving forward because either you can't trust those around you or you don't trust the possibility that things could work out for you.

However, you know (or are learning) what you believe in, what you are devoted to, and what sense of faith will carry you through. This card teaches that spiritual support is real and tangible. The Hanged Man is thought by some to be hanging from the Tree of Life, suggesting that no matter how hard or how far you fall, you are still in the universe and the universe will catch you.

The Hanged Man's upside-down perspective is unconventional. From your perspective, which is based in spiritual rather than worldly truths, you see what others can't. You see beyond illusions and mainstream paradigms to creative solutions, love, beauty, and the divine. Your unconventional perspective may be unsettling or aggravating to some, who may retaliate with condemnation and persecution. However, you are on your path to the ultimate freedom, attainment, and celebration.

Reversed

Reversed, The Hanged Man indicates hang-ups and injustices that plague your spirit, convincing you to lose trust in yourself or in the divine. The reversed Hanged Man can indicate despair that comes from being separated from your beliefs and truths. While the upright Hanged Man can be a card of self-sacrifice in the name of one's beliefs and convictions, this card reversed asks if you have been sacrificing yourself out of habit. Search deep within for your faith. It is there, and it is one thing you can trust to truly hold and support you.

Symbolism

TREE Tree of Life

HALO Enlightenment

BLUE SHIRT Intuition

RED PANTS Vitality, fearlessness

Mystic Meanings

As a figure who is paused and waiting, The Hanged Man exists beyond time, suspended in timeless truths. In numerology, the number 12 gestures to time—the year divided into 12 months and into 12 signs of the zodiac—and the fact that The Hanged Man may be able to see all of time at once.

The Hanged Man's element is water, indicating a spiritual and emotional time.

The Hanged Man is associated with Neptune, the planet of subtlety and spiritual perception.

Supporting and Opposing Cards

Along with The Hanged Man, the Two of Swords emphasizes a time of pause to go inward to connect with intuitive truths. The Hermit's wisdom emphasizes that of The Hanged Man.

Posing a Question

I don't feel supported by my family. Am I doing something wrong?

It's important to understand the reasons you feel unsupported have nothing to do with anything you have "done wrong." Pulling The Hanged Man indicates that you tend to act with an awareness of a reality beyond this one and with a belief in the divine. You may frequently question your own spiritual perceptions, but it's important to understand that your family feels unsure of how to react to your truths and inner freedom. Continue to believe what you believe, as doubt will get you nowhere.

Trust is an important issue for The Hanged Man. Do what you can to foster trust between yourself and your family. Help them understand you, and remain open and curious about them and how you all can connect.

The Hierophant's conventions and institutions clash with The Hanged Man's unconventional, creative, or iconoclastic truths. Cards of speed, urgency, and outward action—such as the Knight of Swords—detract from The Hanged Man's inward journey and subtle, inner convictions.

DEATH.

ALSO KNOWN AS Transformation

KEYWORDS Endings, Grief, Transformation, Rebirth

ELEMENT Water

ASTROLOGY Scorpio

NUMEROLOGY 13, Reduces to 4

Death is a card of endings, grief, and letting go. When we let go, we transform. Fear breaks down, unleashing love.

The death that has occurred in this card is the death of a king. We see that his crown has been knocked off. Death suggests that we may have lost a degree of control, but, as we learned in The Hanged Man, we don't have to hold ourselves up all the time. Even when we lose the ability to control a situation, we can find trust in the divine. It is possible that we've secretly been longing to be free from a certain inner control mechanism that, possibly due to sorrowful circumstances, we are now released from.

The Death card reminds us that death doesn't mean one particular thing. The child in this card faces death with wide-eyed curiosity. The maiden turns away from death and laments. The bishop greets death solemnly. Just as the figures in the card each relate to death differently, none of us can predict what an ending will mean to us or how it will feel. This card, therefore, reminds us not to preemptively fear endings just because they are endings.

If you have pulled the Death card and fear the ending it represents, be patient with yourself in your fear, and remember to look beyond the fear to see the whole story. Death is a card of liberation and rebirth. Growth can be painful, but it is always worth it. Who do you want to become? What is the world you wish to live in? Believe in your transformation.

Reversed

Death, reversed, suggests that you are refusing to accept an ending. You fall prey to worry, fear, and confusion, resisting your own transformation. Remember that you cannot control anything about this ending except for the amount that you grow from it and the beauty you make from your pain.

Symbolism

ROSICRUCIAN ROSE The four elements and quintessence, or spirit (emphasized as central in this symbol)

KING'S CROWN Control

DEATH'S BLACK ARMOR Protection

RIVER River Styx, the soul's journey after death

Mystic Meanings

In numerology, the number 13 is not an unlucky number; rather, it is a powerful number indicating the ability to confront truth and thereby transform. When the digits are added together, the number 13 reduces to 4, echoing The Emperor's acceptance of reality's hard facts. The stability of the number 4 offers us a feeling of resolution.

Death's element, water, allows us to release our grief and pain through tears, helping us cleanse our spirit.

Death's astrological association is Scorpio. Scorpios are fascinated by transformation, sometimes causing the death of a false way of thinking or being. Scorpios are calm in the face of change.

Posing a Question

I've always enjoyed being around people, but recently I've been experiencing anxiety in groups. What is underlying my fear?

If you have pulled the Death card in answer to this question, your identity (your armor) is in flux. You feel tender, but you are resilient, formed by coming through fire. Be gentle with yourself. Know that your sensitivity is due to getting used to your new self. Focus on the growth you must do, rather than temporary solutions for your anxiety. Time will soothe your self-consciousness, and you will once again enjoy being with others.

Supporting and Opposing Cards

If the Ten of Swords comes up in a reading along with Death, the cards are acknowledging the pain you are experiencing due to an ending. Be sure to acknowledge the emotional impact of this situation so that you can grieve and heal. The Wheel of Fortune emphasizes an ending that is fated or beyond your control. Don't guilt yourself about this ending. Instead, learn from what has happened, and move forward with a positive attitude.

There is no card that negates Death. The Fool, however, may be oblivious or blasé in the face of an important ending.

ALSO KNOWN AS Art

KEYWORDS Creativity, Art, Healing, Balance

ELEMENT Fire

ASTROLOGY Sagittarius

NUMEROLOGY 14, Reduces to 5

Temperance allows us to flourish emotionally, creatively, and spiritually, due to having all the elements of our life flowing together in harmonious balance. Temperance is the card of alchemy, art, and metaphors. It is about elements combining to heal an imbalance and create an experience that is more than the sum of its parts. The angel in this card pours water from a silver cup to a gold cup, combining elements. The water magically pours sideways, indicating that, in the creative zone, the impossible becomes possible.

This card's definition of temperance is not abstinence, but rather the right balance of elements. This principle is represented by the placement of the angel's feet: one on land, one in water. If you have pulled Temperance, you are encouraged to find or maintain balance. If you are struggling with addiction or imbalance, instead of forcing yourself to abstain from something, make improvements in other areas of your life so that they will provide you with the satisfaction you are looking for. Temper yourself by *adding* a practice or experience to your day, which is intrinsically fulfilling and helps balance out any destructive behaviors or influences.

Reversed

Temperance, reversed, indicates a lack of balance. This imbalance may be caused by indulgence or addiction, or else by deprivation, as in eating disorders or the rejection of your own emotions. Take steps to restore balance.

Symbolism

ANGEL Divine protection

WATER Purification, healing

THE SEPTENARY (TRIANGLE WITHIN A SQUARE)
Seven principals of human experience

IRISES Hope

Mystic Meanings

In numerology, the number 14 signals stability. As such, it indicates that emotions are not primary in the inspired state, but rather one of many qualities present. When the digits are added together, the number 14 reduces to 5, a dynamic number of change and mediation. This echoes Temperance's meaning of combining many different elements.

Temperance's element is fire. This is a dynamic card in which elements are combined and creative or fiery chemical reactions take place.

The zodiac sign Sagittarius is associated with Temperance. People born under Sagittarius have many varied interests but are also very direct. Similarly, Temperance combines unique elements with specific aims in mind.

Posing a Question

I'm working under a tight deadline. What quality will help me complete my project on time?

If you have pulled Temperance in response to a quality you need to channel in order to help you achieve a goal, you are encouraged to find balance to successfully complete your task. Stay healthy through the big push of your deadline by nourishing yourself, getting enough sleep, and refraining from isolating yourself. Allow the flow of your creativity to guide and fuel you.

Supporting and Opposing Cards

The Star in combination with Temperance emphasizes Temperance's meaning of healing. Balance is emphasized by the Two of Cups and Justice.

The Fives of Wands and the Five of Swords indicate chaos and conflict, respectively. They both oppose the harmony of Temperance. The Devil's hedonism opposes Temperance's balance.

THE DEVIL.

ALSO KNOWN AS Pan, Temptation, Captor of the Lost

KEYWORDS Vitality, Play, Temptation, Oppression

ELEMENT Earth

ASTROLOGY Capricorn

NUMEROLOGY 15, Reduces to 6

The devil figure in this card is the Greek god Pan. Half-goat, half-man, Pan was a revered god of nature, lust, play, and other pleasures of the flesh, such as music and food. In the fourth century, Christian theologians began to demonize Pan, adding goat horns to depictions of Satan. In the tarot, The Devil retains elements of playful, lusty, vital Pan, but also depicts what happens when materialism gets the best of us.

The Devil encourages us to look at what seems inappropriate in our lives, either within ourselves or in situations we find ourselves part of. If you have pulled The Devil, you are asked to look closer at your mischievousness and sense of play. Are you being playful or provocative when it comes to rules and bondage? Are you bringing levity to grave situations, breaking down barriers and unnecessary rules to allow for pleasure and fun? What vital energy is coursing through you?

On the other hand, are you causing harm? Is this inappropriateness a case of manipulation or oppression, either by you or against you? Are you repressing, rejecting, or shaming any part of yourself or others? What are the dynamics of this situation? Is there a way to bring about freedom?

Another aspect of The Devil is that we sometimes believe we are trapped when, in fact, we are not. The chains around the necks of The Devil's minions are loose. They could take them off if they wanted. As shown on the card, they are chained by manipulation, greed, and their fears of taking responsibility for the negative aspects of themselves. They blame each other or The Devil for their negative actions. The Devil card asks us to face our fears and our shadow sides to free ourselves from their control.

Reversed

Reversed, The Devil signifies release and severance, freeing yourself, finding that you are not as trapped as you first thought you were.

Symbolism

DEVIL Pan, nature, bodily pleasure

MAN AND WOMAN Adam and Eve, condemned due to their susceptibility to temptation

INVERTED PENTACLE Cruelty

CHAINS Being trapped, either by choice or through manipulation or oppression

Mystic Meanings

In numerology, the number 15 signifies imprisonment and antagonism. When the digits are added together, this reduces to 6. The couple depicted may look familiar—they also appear in The Lovers. The number 15 reveals the shadows and power struggles on the flip side of the harmony and passivity of The Lovers' number 6.

The half-goat figures of the zodiac sign Capricorn and The Devil are indefatigable creatures. They wield energy and strength, but both can get caught in their own negative expectations. Associated with the earth, they carry grounding, though potentially heavy, energy, pointing to the challenge of loosening their perspective so they can play.

Posing a Question

What is causing all this chaos in my life?

Pulling The Devil card in answer to this question can indicate a situation in which you feel trapped. Sometimes, pulling this card may mean that you have been putting up with a domineering partner, boss, roommate, or landlord—often due to financial constraints. The cause of the chaos in your life is likely due to real or imagined constraints that compel you to stay in an unhealthy situation. Ask yourself what keeps you in the impossible situations you're involved in. Consider if these constraints are real; If they are real, brainstorm how you could creatively or strategically escape them. Remember that The Devil's other characteristic is playfulness. See if you can play your way out of these situations.

Supporting and Opposing Cards

The Nine of Cups combined with The Devil emphasizes overindulgence. The crisis of The Moon suggests an inner reckoning with Devilish base instincts, such as greed or a need for dominance.

The moderation of Temperance contrasts with The Devil's hedonistic overindulgence and power-hungry restriction or oppression of others.

THE TOWER.

When something in our life isn't working—a habit, a job, a relationship—but we refuse to acknowledge the issues, we build an increasingly precarious tower held together with temporary solutions, wishful thinking, and denial. If we neither take the initiative to dismantle nor restore the shoddy tower, it will inevitably come crashing down.

The Tower signifies a time of total destruction. The foundations we've relied upon, however dysfunctional, have been ripped out from underneath us. Freefalling, we may feel terror or despair.

If you have pulled The Tower, the gift here is that real solutions and solid foundations can be put in place now that an untenable situation is no longer sapping your energy. The Hindu deity Kali—the mother goddess who, out of love, destroys what doesn't work—has rid you of your own poison. Now is a time to purge, detox, and start afresh.

Reversed

Reversed, The Tower indicates that you are affected by someone else's experience of destruction and collapse in their own life. You are spiritually, mentally, and emotionally stronger than this situation, however. Others' mistakes do not have to limit your spirit.

ALSO KNOWN AS The Fire, The Thunderbolt,

KEYWORDS Destruction, Consequences, Catastrophe, Detoxification

ELEMENT Fire

ASTROLOGY Mars

NUMEROLOGY 16, Reduces to 7

Symbolism

CROWN Control

TOWER Fear

LIGHTNING Enlightenment

FLAMES Change, destruction, rebirth

Mystic Meanings

In numerology, the number 16 is actually a positive one, signaling the release of pent-up feelings and a flow of creativity and love. When the digits are added together, the number 16 reduces to 7, the number of spirituality and tests, and resonates with the seventh card in the Major Arcana, The Chariot, a card of breakthrough.

The Tower's element is, unsurprisingly, fire. Fire illuminates that which it destroys. Through the act of destroying what does not work, The Tower both illuminates our learning and releases trapped energy, which we can now harness in order to act upon our learning.

Mars is the planet associated with The Tower. Mars is aggressive, but it is also passionate and sexual. When the tower of our fears and egotism breaks, our passion and vitality are released.

Posing a Question

I got fired from my job and feel like a failure. What do I do now?

If you have pulled The Tower in answer to this question, explore the part of you that was secretly wishing to be free from this job. Focus on that part of your soul. Love that part of you. Now is the time to listen to that part of you that you had to shut out to stay in your job. Allow this passionate, energetic aspect of yourself to come back to life and fuel a new path of positive changes. The rest is water under the bridge.

Supporting and Opposing Cards

The Death card is also a card of endings. When it appears along with The Tower, an all-encompassing transformation is undeniably taking place. The Ten of Swords combined with The Tower emphasizes the violence of all that comes crashing to an end in The Tower.

If combined with The Star, Temperance, or The Chariot, the upheaval of The Tower is mitigated by a feeling of release and a new sense of purpose.

ALSO KNOWN AS Star of Wonder, The Stars, Hope

KEYWORDS Guiding Vision, Healing, Creativity

ELEMENT Air

ASTROLOGY Aquarius

NUMEROLOGY 17, Reduces to 8

Just as the stars can be used for navigation, The Star is our guiding vision or ideal that will always point us in the right direction. No matter how far we may be from reaching our vision, we know we are on the right path when we are heading toward it.

The Star helps us believe in miracles and allows us to connect with the magic of every day. The ibis in this card represents the Egyptian god Thoth. As the god of thought, language, and magic, Thoth reminds us of the power of our thoughts and words. The things we name are potent. Naming our ideals can breathe life into them. Our experience is rich with beauty and meaning.

If you have pulled The Star, now is a time for healing and rejuvenation. Offer yourself grounding and cleansing rituals. It is okay to face the naked truth of your vulnerability right now; you are beautiful, and you deserve to heal.

Be sure that your ritual, healing, and ideals are as grounding as they are purifying. At an extreme, The Star indicates naïveté. Don't get lost in visions of the future. Set goals and intentions that are personal, rather than abstract. Open yourself to awe in your daily life and relationships. You are an inspiration to many people.

Reversed

Reversed, The Star indicates naïveté and obliviousness. Are you relying on belief to the extent that your idealism replaces taking actual action toward your ideals? Alternately, your sense of hope, idealism, and possibility are latent. You or others are ignoring the solutions and remedies that are possible if you allow yourself to hope and believe.

Symbolism

STAR Guiding light

POURING WATER Purification, healing

WATER AND EARTH Balance, grounding, and spirituality

IBIS Thoth, language, magic

NAKEDNESS Purity, honesty

MOUNTAINS Aspirations

Mystic Meanings

In numerology, the number 17 indicates quiet certainty, subtle strength. When the digits are added together, the number 17 reduces to 8, the number of strength. Your visions are strong, and you have the strength and perceptiveness necessary to carry through.

The Star's element is air. This card unburdens us, uplifts us. We are able to feel a lightness of heart and spirit that may have previously eluded us.

In astrology, The Star is associated with the zodiac sign Aquarius. Aquarius people naturally inspire others with their idealism and their belief in possibility. The Star represents a person, situation, or ideal that fills you with a feeling of optimism.

Posing a Question

I'm grieving the loss of a loved one. What will comfort me in my days of mourning?

If you pull The Star, a positive and inspired card, in answer to this question, it suggests you focus on the way your loved one can continue to be a guiding light for you and others. Spend time considering the visions this person had for the world. What did they inspire in those around them? What did they inspire in you? Honor your loved one by dedicating yourself to integrating these inspirations into the way you live your life. Think about how you can spread the light of your loved one's energy.

Supporting and Opposing Cards

Temperance supports The Star, emphasizing balance, healing, and cleansing. The Six of Swords also supports The Star, emphasizing calmness.

The Tower, on the other hand, as well as the Nine of Swords, opposes The Star, suggesting that your glimpses of hope arrive amidst a time of upheaval and worry. Also, The Devil's overindulgence and power imbalance, in combination with The Star, suggest idealism that is overwrought, indulgent, or forced upon others.

THE MOON.

ALSO KNOWN AS Illusion

KEYWORDS Dreams, Instinct, Crisis

ELEMENT Water

ASTROLOGY Pisces

NUMEROLOGY 18, Reduces to 9

The Moon indicates experiences that take place under the light of the moon or in the subconscious. Dreams, trespasses, sexuality, animal instincts and fears, confusion, illusion, crimes, and moments of internal crisis all lie within the realm of The Moon.

The wolf and dog howling at the moon in this card express the fine, yet important, line between domesticity and wildness. The image of the moon represents our instincts and our animal nature. It affirms our intuition, dreams, and spirituality, but also indicates our capacity for cruelty.

Our instincts often run on fear, represented here by the two windowless towers, fortresses of entrapment and the unknown. What did it take for us to become domesticated? How, in childhood, was cruelty used to tame our wildness?

The Moon, at its worst, can represent codependent or abusive relationship patterns learned in childhood and other terrible certainties, such as deep-set illusions of aloneness and expectations of violence, that reside in the core of our consciousness. If you have pulled The Moon, you may be experiencing a crisis of faith or a dark night of the soul—but also your animalistic survival instinct and drive that will pull you through to meet the daylight.

Reversed

When The Moon is reversed, rather than exploring your subconscious, you ignore it. Your gut is giving you signs, but you keep tamping down your intuition, getting yourself into trouble. Emotions are building up, but you are not letting them out. Trauma feels so overwhelming you don't even consider the possibility of healing. It is time to start finding ways to heal. Otherwise, continued depression or a rude awakening is in store. It is possible for you to regain your flow.

Symbolism

WOLF Instinct

DOG Domesticated wildness

COMBINED SUN AND MOON Duality of action or volition, and reflection or receptivity

CRAYFISH Primordial self, aquatic origins

TOWERS, WATCHTOWERS Fears; together they guard the line between the subconscious and consciousness

LONG WINDING PATH An unknown destination

Mystic Meanings

In numerology, the number 18 represents gentle exploration of vulnerability and the unknown, of hidden matters unfolding. When the digits are added together, the number 18 reduces to 9, a number of meditation, abundance, and achieving goals.

The Moon's element is water. Water represents the expression of emotions, as well as the malleability and fluidity of our consciousness.

Posing a Question

Why do I keep finding myself in unhealthy relationships?

If you have pulled The Moon in response to this question, you are encouraged to look deeply at old patterns embedded since childhood in your subconscious understanding of the world. Seek support, and be gentle with yourself. Old wounds cut deep, but you are strong and willing to heal. Recognizing and learning about your wounds is more than half the struggle. There will be sunnier days ahead.

The Moon's astrological link is to the zodiac sign Pisces. Pisces folks value healing, intuition, intimacy, and boundaries. The Moon similarly encompasses the fluidness of boundaries, teaching us the sometimes subtle differences between intimacy and violence, and helping us heal our boundaries.

Supporting and Opposing Cards

Combined with The Hermit, The Moon offers you a time of solitude, reflection, and intuition.

The Emperor's stability opposes The Moon's fluidity. This combination can signify an unpredictable leader or conflict between stability and fluidity.

THE SUN.

ALSO KNOWN AS The Children

KEYWORDS Joy, Success, Health, Children

ELEMENT Fire

ASTROLOGY The Sun

NUMEROLOGY 19, Reduces to 10 and 1

On a sunny day when the weather is just right, we often can't help but feel joyful. The Sun represents the joy that the sun naturally brings to us. If you have pulled The Sun, you may feel as unguarded and gleeful as the child depicted in this card.

This card suggests that the sun has come out after a difficult time, such as illness. The sun's illumination clears up confusion, restores us to health, and dispels danger and resentment. You are now able to enjoy visibility. This is a time of success, recognition, and love. You may enjoy awards, prosperity, a joyful marriage, children, or grandchildren. A symbol of consciousness, The Sun shows you acting with confidence, conviction, and awareness.

Perhaps most important, The Sun indicates that you are easily able to give and receive compassion. The way we instinctually love and help a child, who unquestioningly receives our support, compassion is a reflex for you. Gratitude is foundational for you. You have the resources, successes, and support you need, and you are therefore able to extend your compassion and clarity to those who could use some more love.

Reversed

Oftentimes, the reversed meaning of The Sun is the same as its upright definition. Occasionally, however, the reversal suggests the loss of, or difficulties concerning, something cherished. Keep an eye out for trouble, and change course if necessary.

Symbolism

CHILD Happiness, honesty, innocence, wholeness, inner child

SUNFLOWERS Growth, beauty, and spiritual attainment

RED FLAG Vitality

GARDEN WALL Peacefulness and safety

HORSE The body

Mystic Meanings

In numerology, the number 19 represents attainment and clarity triumphing over uncertainty. When the digits are added together, the number 19 reduces to 10, the number of beginnings (in this case, children) and endings (the joyful success being celebrated). Then 10 reduces to 1, the number of unity, beginnings, and power.

The Sun's element is fire, emphasizing its energy, vitality, warmth, and power to illuminate.

The Sun's astrological association is the sun itself. The sun gives us health, clarity, and energy. It suggests that The Sun's qualities—joy, compassion, health, and success—are neither optional nor rare, but rather come up daily and

> ## Posing a Question
>
> *My brother invited me to visit him overseas, and I'm uncertain of our current relationship dynamics. What's the likely outcome if I accept?*
>
> When The Sun is pulled in answer to this question, it indicates that the foundation of your relationship with your brother is joy. If your brother has a child or children, they will further add joy to your life if you choose to visit. If you make the journey, the connection and fun you have on this trip will continue to light your days long after you return home.

regularly enjoy their season to shine. Pay attention to the simple, fundamental joys in your life. They are as real and important as anything else.

Supporting and Opposing Cards

Cards whose meanings include enjoying time with family or loved ones, such as the Nine of Cups, heighten The Sun's happiness. So do cards of success and achievement, such as The World or the Six of Wands.

Gloomy or anxious cards, like The Tower and the Nine of Swords, overshadow The Sun.

JUDGEMENT.

ALSO KNOWN AS The Last Judgment, The Angel

KEYWORDS Higher Calling, Criticism, Judgment Call, Absolution

ELEMENT Fire

ASTROLOGY Pluto

NUMEROLOGY 20, Reduces to 2

The Judgement card signals that we have changed in some deep way. Archangel Gabriel's trumpet calls us to fully awaken to this change. By card 20 in the Fool's Journey of the Major Arcana, we have experienced nearly every major type of human experience. We are now able to accept a higher calling.

Even under judgment, the naked figures in this card do not feel vulnerable. They have no more secrets. They feel awe, amazement, and the energy of their own and each other's awakening.

If you have pulled Judgement, you are going through a rite of passage. This rite of passage readies you to progress to the final achievement of this go around of your Fool's Journey. A divine judgment call is being made upon your actions and growth.

Or perhaps you are being called upon to make a judgment call. Critical thinking is important at this time, but be careful of being overly critical. At its extreme, Judgement indicates an excessively critical mind-set that inhibits us from succeeding.

The Judgement card represents forgiveness, release, and the celebration of a new life as we rise to a higher calling.

Reversed

Reversed, Judgement suggests that you are being overly critical and thereby killing any possibility of spiritual awakening. Make an effort to be less critical and see what opens up for you.

Symbolism

ARCHANGEL GABRIEL Divine messenger

TRUMPET Announcement of a decision

RED CROSS Rescue, health, healing

CHILD Newly reborn consciousness

NAKEDNESS Purity, honesty

Mystic Meanings

In numerology, the number 20 represents unity and reconciling of conflicts or challenges. This reduces to 2, the number of balance and choice. The ill-informed choices we have made throughout our Fool's Journey are, we hope, now balanced by the growth we've achieved. If not, a divine judge is balancing things for us, throwing us one last task to overcome in order to solidify and integrate the lessons we initially set out to learn.

Judgement's element is fire, which burns up impurities.

Judgement's astrological association is Pluto, the planet of soul-deep transformation.

Supporting and Opposing Cards

The Lovers emphasize Judgement's meaning of a higher calling. Temperance and The Star reinforce Judgement's qualities of release, renewal, and cleansing.

In the Judgement card, we are well beyond cards of beginnings and potential, such as the Aces or The Fool, which diffuse Judgement's potency.

Posing a Question

I don't think the project I've been working on is going anywhere. What would be the consequences of starting over?

If you have pulled Judgement in answer to this question, you are likely nearing the end of your project, and your desire to quit is actually a desire to avoid judgment—both from the outside world about the quality of your work, as well as a reluctance to face what you need to face to get through to the end of your project.

The Judgement card suggests that even if you change projects, you will still have to face whatever it is that has been staring you down in the final stages of the current project. You're at a time in your life when it is especially important to face yourself and the quality of your contributions to the world.

Likely, the thing that feels incorrect or missing in your project is an ingredient that is also missing in your life. What you discover by either finishing this project or starting it anew will be just the wake-up call you have been waiting for.

THE WORLD.

ALSO KNOWN AS The Universe

KEYWORDS Completion, Celebration, Wholeness

ELEMENT Earth

ASTROLOGY Saturn

NUMEROLOGY 21, Reduces to 3

The World is a card of completing a project or journey, and coming full circle. This completion might be a birthday, graduation, anniversary, retirement, or other milestone.

Themes of this card include unity and wholeness. The figure dancing in this card is an intersex person who embodies a spectrum of possibility and expression. If you have pulled The World, feelings of arrival, acceptance, and belonging pervade your life.

The World is a card of celebration and dancing for joy. After a long, intense journey—the Fool's Journey—of challenges and learning, you can finally enjoy your success, mastery, achievement, and rewards!

Reversed

Reversed, The World indicates the need to work within limitations. Boundaries have been set for you, which are, for the current moment, nonnegotiable. Still, it is possible for you to find freedom within your circumstances. Doing so will not only bring you joy, but your ability to bring your freedom with you into any circumstance will be an excellent skill to carry forward.

Symbolism

CHERUB, EAGLE, LION, BULL Fixed signs of the zodiac (Aquarius, Scorpio, Leo, Taurus), four elements (air, water, fire, earth), four directions (north, south, east, west), four phases of life (infancy, youth, adulthood, old age)

DANCING Moving through life and through change with understanding, love, creativity, and energy; aligning your inner being with your outer actions

LEMNISCATES (SIDEWAYS FIGURE 8S HOLDING THE WREATH TOGETHER) Infinity

LAUREL WREATH Victory, power

MAGIC WANDS Channeling thought into creative action

Mystic Meanings

In numerology, the number 21 indicates imagination and social giftedness. When the digits are added together, the number 21 reduces to 3, The Empress's number of creativity and life. We have brought a project of The Empress's boundless creativity to full completion for the social good of many people.

The World's element is, predictably, earth. We stand strong on firm, solid ground. We are supported by loved ones and, in turn, are able to support them. We embody our connection to the whole. We know who we are and what we stand for.

In astrology, The World card is linked to the planet Saturn. Saturn is conservative and hardworking, making sure that every detail is correct, reinforced, and fortified. Saturn assures us that a success like the one indicated by The World has been no small feat in the making and that our growth and success are solid and sure.

Posing a Question

How can I best support my college-bound daughter?

The World is a card of completion and celebration. Rather than focusing on giving your daughter all the advice you can for her years ahead, take the time to look back with her over her life, how much she has grown, and who she has become. Celebrating her growth and her completion of high school will allow her to enter college with the assurance and confidence she needs to make her own decisions with self-respect and joy. Pulling The World in response to any question about any change or transition suggests that the life change is due to growth, and the transition is in many ways a situation coming full circle.

Supporting and Opposing Cards

Cards of success, achievement, or celebration all emphasize the positive energy of The World. These include The Sun, The Chariot, the Four of Wands, and the Nine of Cups.

Painful cards, such as the Five of Cups, the Ten of Swords, or The Tower, undercut the joy of The World.

THE MINOR ARCANA: CUPS

THE CUPS REPRESENT OUR EMOTIONAL AND SPIRITUAL LIVES. They illuminate our relationships, our love, and our open, receptive, reflective side. They also illuminate issues related to creative flow, and they help us connect with and understand our sources of inspiration. This suit is associated with the element of water.

ACE OF CUPS

NUMBER 1 Oneness, Beginnings, Power

ASTROLOGY Water Signs—Cancer, Scorpio, Pisces

KEYWORDS Love, Joy, Spirituality

The Ace of Cups signifies an overflow of love and joy. The fountains pouring from the cup represent the potential limitlessness of love, as long as you stay open and dedicate yourself to giving and receiving love.

Aces are full of possibility; the Ace of Cups reveals possibilities for expanding your heart and feeling more joy. The Ace of Cups indicates that you are receptive to intuition, love, and life. You feel emotionally, spiritually, and even physically healthy and fertile—which is appropriate, as this card can also indicate pregnancy.

Reversed

Ace of Cups, reversed, suggests hindrances to spiritual growth caused by being too literal about your practice of religion or spirituality, ignoring the spirit of love and generosity—for example, getting hung up on unrealistic ideas of purity or focusing on appearing pious or kind without actually acting with humility or kindness. The Ace of Cups, reversed, can also reveal creative, emotional, spiritual, or physical infertility. Find ways to trust yourself.

Symbolism

CHALICE Receptivity

WATER LILIES Spiritual perfection

WHITE DOVE Peace

EUCHARIST WAFER ENTERING CHALICE
Communion or spark of life entering the womb

RIGHT HAND The giving hand, offering you a gift

W OR M (ZIGZAG SHAPE) Water

THREE BELLS Body, mind, and spirit

TWO OF CUPS

NUMBER 2 Duality, Balance, Choice, Partnership

ASTROLOGY Venus in Cancer

KEYWORDS Partnership, Friendship, Cooperation

The couple pictured on the Two of Cups represents any two people who complement one another in some way, whether as friends, coworkers, or soul mates. The elements of attraction, cooperation, harmony, and balance are guiding you.

You are bringing the unbounded love of the Ace of Cups into your actual relationships and interactions. This card can herald the beginning of a new relationship or a deeper commitment within a current relationship.

ACE OF CUPS

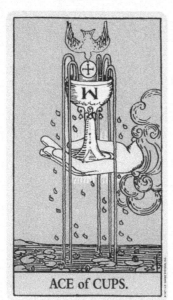

TWO OF CUPS

THREE OF CUPS

Reversed

Reversed, the Two of Cups suggests a loss of balance in relationship caused by miscommunication. If a relationship in your life is harboring distrust, conflict, or tension, restore balance and other upright meanings of this card by communicating openly. It is likely that both parties would rather resolve the issue than continue to fight. The reversed Two of Cups can also signify codependency. How can boundaries and trust be nurtured right now?

Symbolism

LION'S HEAD Vitality, protection through union

CADUCEUS OF HERMES (SNAKES ENTWINED AROUND WINGED POLE) Negotiation, balance in communication

WREATH Success, peace

ROSE WREATH Love, passion

THREE OF CUPS

NUMBER 3 Synthesis, Creativity, Dynamic Balance

ASTROLOGY Mercury in Cancer

KEYWORDS Celebration, Friendship, Camaraderie

The Three of Cups is a celebration among a close-knit group of friends or family. The figures in this card are toasting one another to their friendship or to a group effort. This card can suggest that you have found this group—your people, your tribe, your community. You've finally landed in a caring, meaningful group of like-minded people.

The Three of Cups can also indicate your social or family group as a resource to go to for encouragement at this time. Or this card might point to something important happening within your close social circle: an emotional breakthrough for one of the members of the group, a new member joining the group, or anything else, usually joyful, that one of the members is experiencing, which emotionally affects the whole group.

Reversed

The Three of Cups, reversed, suggests you may be relying too much on your social group or celebrating something prematurely. This might be to distract yourself from something you would rather not be doing or from emotional or sexual dissatisfaction elsewhere in your life. Or you might be spending too much energy on seeking approval within the group. Be sure to address the root cause of the issues in your life so that you are more able to respect and honor the blessings of your friendships.

Symbolism

GOURD Health and vitality

GRAPES Abundance, festivity

YELLOW Friendship, joy

RED Vitality

WHITE Purity

FOUR OF CUPS

NUMBER 4 Material Achievement, Structure, Order

ASTROLOGY Moon in Cancer

KEYWORDS Rest, Reflection, Boredom, Apathy

After the celebration of the Three of Cups, it can be time to take a break and spend some time alone. The Four of Cups can indicate a time of reflecting, daydreaming, meditating, and quietude. Like the figure in this card, seated under a tree during peaceful weather, you enjoy a rest. However, if you stay in this state of mind too long, you can become stagnated and bored. You may feel restless yet uninterested in taking action to change your situation. Just as the figure in this card doesn't acknowledge the goblet being offered to them, you ignore opportunities.

The advice of this card is to enjoy a break without slowing down so much or stepping back so far that you become apathetic—a state from which it is difficult to return without a rude awakening, as you will see in the Five of Cups.

Reversed

Reversed, the Four of Cups signifies a readiness to reengage with your life, to start saying yes again, even to new relationships. The reversal of this card signifies moving on. If you are feeling extremely dissatisfied with your life, name what you would like to change. Accept invitations. Embrace your own ability to make your life wonderful.

Symbolism

CROSSED LEGS AND ARMS Saying no to opportunities and offers

TREE Protection

BLUE SKY Clear mind

FIVE OF CUPS

NUMBER 5 Change, Challenge, Uncertainty, Mediation

ASTROLOGY Mars in Scorpio

KEYWORDS Grief, Sorrow, Mourning

The figure in the Five of Cups mourns three spilt cups while two cups remain upright behind their back. This person gazes down at the cups and across the river, toward the home they have lost or left behind. Fixated on their lost home, the figure in this card has yet to see the fulfillment that awaits once they turn away from their past to see it. After a necessary period of mourning, time will allow the figure to see beyond their sorrows, and they will be able to see the joy and meaning still in their life.

The Five of Cups suggests that you have experienced a deeply painful loss of love, home, job, security, or status. You may have lost a loved one, suffered a breakup, or lost faith in a close friend. Your grief is undeniable. Express your grief or repressed feelings. You may find yourself returning to a childhood or family home. Know that sometimes it takes the Five of Cups to jolt us out of the period of emotional stagnation represented by the Four of Cups. Grieve your loss, and prepare to reconcile yourself with what's left.

Reversed

Reversed, the pain of the Five of Cups intensifies. Your loss feels overwhelming, and healing may feel impossible. Bear with this time. Not all is as lost as it seems. The other meaning of the reversed Five of Cups is that you have come a long way in healing from a loss. You are actively reconciling your past pain with your present life. You may also be receiving new support that helps you face or move on from your loss.

Symbolism

SPILT BLOOD Loss of life, harm to the body

SPILT WATER Loss of spirit

GRAY SKY Uncertainty

SIX OF CUPS

NUMBER 6 Harmony, Integration, Passivity

ASTROLOGY Sun in Scorpio

KEYWORDS Childhood Comforts, Nostalgia

The Six of Cups represents the coziness and comforts of childhood. Like the children in this card, who are playing in the garden, you are experiencing a sweet time of gentle compassion, happiness, and love. You are enjoying the harmony and restfulness denoted by the number 6.

You might be feeling nostalgic and revisiting childhood friends, songs, happy memories, or places that were important to you when you were young. As a teacher, parent, or caregiver, you might be creating this feeling for the children in your life. Children might be especially present or important in your life right now. They also help you stay connected with your own childhood or inner child.

Reversed

If you fall too deeply into the qualities of the Six of Cups, you get lost in nostalgia. In the Six of Cups, reversed, you see your past through rose-colored glasses at the expense of your present life. Or you might be visited by unhappy childhood memories. Whether the memories taking up your field of vision are happy or unhappy, it is important to take responsibility for being present in your life and not allow your past to trap you.

Symbolism

TOWER Protection

WHITE FLOWERS Purity of love

SEVEN OF CUPS

NUMBER 7 Spirituality, Tests

ASTROLOGY Venus in Scorpio

KEYWORDS Fantasy, Creativity, Temptation

If you are working on a creative project, the Seven of Cups is a positive card of inspiration and possibility. There are many possibilities open to you, and you are clueing in to the inspirations and ideas that you will manifest in your art. However, be sure that you do, at some point, move on from reveling in the inspiration and actually do the work of creating your art.

If you are not working on a creative project, be aware that the possibilities surrounding you right now are temptations. Each cup in this card offers a different temptation that could lead you off your path. These temptations might be especially enticing to you now because you are at a crossroads in your life and in need of a next step that brings you hope and satisfaction. Practice patience and self-restraint in your decision-making, and don't be misled by fantasies or shortcuts.

Reversed

Reversed, the Seven of Cups emphasizes the delusions latent in the upright meanings. You might be fooled by appearances, idealizing someone or something, and generally choosing to believe fantasy over reality. Alternately, the reversed Seven of Cups can affirm your composure and your ability to resist fantasy. You may have been offered a momentarily tempting opportunity for money, status, or sex, but you chose to delay gratification in favor of a more realistic path.

Symbolism

ATTRACTIVE FACE Lust, romance

SHROUDED FIGURE Higher consciousness, temptation (promises of easy enlightenment)

SNAKE Wisdom or dishonest ambitions

CASTLE Unrealistic hopes (castles in the sky)

FOUR OF CUPS

FIVE OF CUPS

SIX OF CUPS

SEVEN OF CUPS

GEMS Riches

LAUREL WREATH Victory and power

DRAGON WITH BARBED TONGUE
Beguiling dangers

SEVEN CUPS Seven sins or temptations
(lust, rage, gluttony, pride, greed, envy, sloth)

EIGHT OF CUPS

NUMBER 8 Navigation, Prosperity, Authority

ASTROLOGY Saturn in Pisces

KEYWORDS Leaving, Wandering, Seeking

The figure in the Eight of Cups is shown leaving a stable life, represented by eight neatly arranged cups. The figure heads away from their stable life, across a rocky river, toward mysteries hidden in the mountains. The Eight of Cups represents your need for exploration, soul-searching, and growth. Disappointment with your present life or boredom with your achievements may compel you into the unknown in search of more meaning. This calling is often as spiritual as it is inexplicable.

If this card often appears in your readings, it can indicate a habitual compulsion to leave situations and relationships at the first signs of stability or boredom. Consider whether perhaps, this time, staying and combating your own detachment might be the more compelling unknown.

Reversed

The Eight of Cups, reversed, may find you adrift. You may be endlessly traveling, wandering, leaving, and abandoning situations too soon. If you are wandering in search of a home, it may be that you haven't practiced the patience it requires to make a home. Alternately, the reversed Eight of Cups can signify returning home from a spiritual search, either because it is time to integrate what you have learned or because you have given up on your quest.

Symbolism

RED CLOAK AND BOOTS Power, strength

WANING CRESCENT Letting go

FULL MOON Transformation

DARK BLUE SKY Spirituality

ROCKY WATER Mental disturbances

NINE OF CUPS

NUMBER 9 Completion, Meditation, Achievement of Goals

ASTROLOGY Jupiter in Pisces

KEYWORDS Hosting, Welcoming, Enjoyment

The Nine of Cups features a comfortable, contented innkeeper ready to host a night of merriment. This party is about being a welcoming, generous host. You bring friends, family, or community together in the spirit of happiness and unconditional love. This card signifies parties and gatherings that celebrate good company, as compared to the Four of Wands celebration in which a formal achievement is celebrated. You know you deserve to enjoy life because you are alive.

Because the Nine of Cups is about enjoyment and partying, it indicates satisfaction. Ideally, this is a time in which you nourish your soul and extend acceptance and love to the people in your life. If a more superficial experience of this card is being had, your focus might be more on the gratification brought by substances than through substantial relationships. At the extreme, the Nine of Cups indicates feelings of smugness or complacency. Are you throwing a party just to show off? Are you getting so comfortable you forget to be generous or to dedicate yourself to what you care about?

Overall, now is a good time to host a party, enjoy your health, and share your good fortune with those you love.

Reversed

The Nine of Cups, reversed, indicates that either you don't feel you deserve to enjoy yourself or you are overindulging. If you feel undeserving, it might be due to a recent financial or material disappointment, or to an incorrect belief that you don't deserve the experiences you want to have. Try being as generous with yourself as you

are with others. If, however, you are more focused on your material satisfactions and indulgences than you are on the well-being of others, it is time to start sharing more and listening more deeply to those around you.

Symbolism

PLUMPNESS Wealth, satisfaction

YELLOW Joy

RED HAT Affluence

TEN OF CUPS

NUMBER 10 Pinnacle (of Success or Difficulty), Beginnings and Endings

ASTROLOGY Mars in Pisces

KEYWORDS Family Love, Togetherness, Joy

The Ten of Cups represents family, happiness, and living your ideal of family. Your relationships right now are satisfying. Your family or community members value one another as they are, for who they are. This is not a passing moment. The bonds you have made will continue to grow. Within your group of chosen or biological family, communication, love, affirmation, and support will continue to deepen. You are able to love one another well and enjoy your togetherness.

A key to the stability of the familial relationships portrayed in the Ten of Cups is your acceptance of people and situations as they are.

EIGHT OF CUPS

NINE OF CUPS

TEN OF CUPS

While the rainbow is an idealistic symbol of hope and dreams come true, the Ten of Cups indicates your ability to see the love, happiness, and other ideals within your imperfect human relationships. Rather than getting sidetracked pursuing unrealistic ideals, you are living in accordance with the spirit of your familial ideals, allowing for necessary hiccups and flaws.

Reversed

Reversed, the Ten of Cups still indicates love and togetherness. However, there's an issue that requires your attention. What is your ideal of family? Is something or someone disturbing your otherwise harmonious family life? If so, do your best to deal with this issue, prioritizing the well-being of your family or community. Alternately, is it actually your ideal of what family "should" look like that is distracting you from the real joy in your life? If you have gotten sidetracked searching for or trying to enforce an ideal, focus instead on accepting your tribe and loving them for who they are.

Symbolism

RAINBOW Hope, dreams come true, reward

RIVER Fertility

COTTAGE Home

PAGE OF CUPS

ASTROLOGY Water Signs—Cancer, Pisces, Scorpio

KEYWORDS Innocent, Imaginative, Dreamer, Inspiring News

The Page of Cups denotes the discovery of new feelings. Youth, innocence, and harmony are exuded by the Page of Cups. Whether this card refers to you or to someone in your life, the Page of Cups indicates someone who is enchanted by the inspirations they find in their own and others' inner life, and in their emotional connections with others. In the image, we see the Page regarding the fish poking its head out of a cup. The fish represents emotions, intuition, visions, and feelings that have surfaced through creativity, intimacy, dreams, or imagination.

The Page of Cups is a young or youthful poet, artist, or dreamer. The Page of Cups may be a child, young person, or adult who is young in spirit. This person is sensitive, emotional, and intuitive. Generally, they are imaginative and filled with awe. However, the Page of Cups can also indicate naïveté and can suggest that this person may have some growing up to do.

Pages can represent a personality or personality trait, as above, or a message. The Page of

Cups indicates that you might soon receive a message about love or creativity, such as news from a loved one, news of your artwork being well received, or information that brings a new breath of inspiration.

Reversed

Reversed, the Page of Cups indicates someone who is naïve, irresponsible, and impulsive. They are too immersed in their own emotions to notice the people around them. They have either let you down because of this or encourage you to be the same way.

If you find yourself embodying these characteristics, channel the upright qualities of the Page of Cups: creativity, awe, and openness. Use these qualities to help you learn and grow, rather than getting swept up in your ideas about these qualities.

Symbolism

FISH EMERGING FROM CUP Dream figures and emotions emerging from the subconscious; fertility (in Paganism)

WATER LILIES Emotional purity

UNDULATING WAVES Full of emotion

PINK Love

BLUE Spirituality

KNIGHT OF CUPS

ASTROLOGY Aquarius, Pisces

KEYWORDS Romance, Idealism, Passion, Inspiration

The Knight of Cups indicates a romantic, impassioned experience. You might receive a romantic proposal, meet a new romantic partner, travel, make new friends, or get swept up in a creative project.

The Knight of Cups is charming, social, and easy to get along with—at least on the surface. They are idealistic but can get easily hurt or impatient when people or situations challenge their ideals. If you are the Knight of Cups in this reading, consider ways in which you can help your actions live up to your ideas, using your passion to propel you through the awkward trials and errors. If the Knight of Cups refers to a person in your life, enjoy your Knight of Cups' openness, but be aware of whether you can truly trust this person. The Knight of Cups isn't always able to live up to their own ideals.

Anytime a Knight appears in a reading, see if the Knight faces another card. The card the Knight faces can help reveal the direction in which the Knight's energy is directed or the area of life in which you should expect the Knight's energy to manifest.

Reversed

Reversed, the Knight of Cups indicates latent qualities in you or the situation in question; you are holding back from taking action or expressing your emotions. There is a block in your emotional, creative, or spiritual life. This block could be eased by dedicating yourself to expressing your feelings more and taking more action on your ideas.

The root of your block might be a feeling of rejection or disappointment, or fear of rejection. You might insist that your relationships conform to a romantic ideal, afraid to accept a partner with imperfections or afraid to reveal your own flaws. Don't let your fears hold you back from accepting and giving love.

Alternately, the Knight of Cups, reversed, can warn that you or your romantic partner is behaving possessively. Address this issue so that you don't continue to restrict the love in your life.

Symbolism

WINGED ARMOR Hermes, god of messages and communication, traveling, and border crossings

RED FISH Passion

RIVER Fertility, flow of emotions

QUEEN OF CUPS

ASTROLOGY Gemini, Cancer

KEYWORDS Nurturing, Healing

The way the Queen of Cups holds the chalice indicates the reverence she brings to nurturing life. The Queen of Cups may indicate your own loving nature, a mother figure (of any gender), or a time in your life in which your dashed hopes are able to heal.

The Queen of Cups is compassionate. They are able to make the people they talk to feel seen. With understanding, the Queen of Cups nurtures others and helps them grow. This person gracefully holds space for any and all emotions, allowing for great depth of vulnerability. Your experiences with the Queen of Cups—or, if you are the Queen of Cups, the interactions you offer others—are redemptive. The Queen of Cups is a healer, a mother, or anyone who plumbs the depths of experience for the sake of personal and communal growth and love.

Reversed

The reversed Queen of Cups neglects to love herself. She may suffer depression or see herself as a victim. The reversed Queen of Cups can be emotionally manipulative or draining. If this describes you, don't lose sight of who you really

PAGE OF CUPS

KNIGHT OF CUPS

PAGE of CUPS.

KNIGHT of CUPS.

QUEEN of CUPS.

KING of CUPS.

QUEEN OF CUPS

KING OF CUPS

are. Know and trust that people value you for your compassionate, healing, and nurturing qualities.

Symbolism

COVERED GOLDEN CHALICE Womb; spirituality, faith

BABY MERMAIDS Water-babies, children in the womb

PEBBLES Polished bits of wisdom; abundance (indicated by repeated pebble pattern)

KING OF CUPS

ASTROLOGY Libra, Scorpio

KEYWORDS Calm, Shoulder to Cry On

The King of Cups represents emotional balance. Sitting still in a stone throne in an undulating sea, the King of Cups stays calm and collected under pressure. Like the Queen of Cups, the King of Cups is compassionate and unconditional. While the Queen's love is intensely healing, the King's love is more measured, stable, and diplomatic. The King of Cups is a father figure (of any gender) and offers a reassuring shoulder to cry on. Professionally, the King of Cups has become a master in their field by following their intuitive moral compass.

You may be embodying the qualities of the King of Cups or experiencing them in your life—offering or receiving stable, nonjudgmental love, or following your intuition in a calm, measured way—or the card may refer to someone in your life who embodies these qualities. This person may already be part of your life or you may be about to meet them.

The King of Cups must be sure to process and express their emotions regularly with those they trust. Otherwise, they might clamp down too hard on their emotions to maintain the calm demeanor people expect of them. This can lead to stress, aloofness, or shame.

Reversed

Reversed, the King of Cups struggles with insecurity, shame, or hatred. They might turn to an addiction to help them get through the day. At their lowest point, they betray people they love. If this describes you, seek emotional balance.

Symbolism

CONCH SHELL THRONE Strong, stable, protective amidst rough waters; Triton, a Greek sea god

FISH Faith, prosperity, passion

JELLYFISH CROWN Equanimity, as jellyfish rely on the currents to carry them, accepting and trusting the currents

7

THE MINOR ARCANA: PENTACLES

THE PENTACLES IN THEIR MOST LITERAL SENSE ARE COINS.
They represent money, resources, property, land, and the raw
materials we create with. They are concerned with security, home,
and nature. They represent commerce and work, and particularly
work associated directly with land, property, or resources, such
as farmers, vendors, and sculptors. The element associated with
Pentacles is earth.

ACE OF PENTACLES

NUMBER 1 Oneness, Beginnings, Power

ASTROLOGY Earth Signs—Taurus, Virgo, Capricorn

KEYWORDS Perfection, Contentment, Prosperity

The Ace of Pentacles represents prosperity, possibility, and the beginning of a new life. This new life can be a literal birth or a new lease on life that arrives as the result of getting a promotion, starting a new career, moving into a new home, or receiving an unexpected gift, treasure, or windfall.

As a symbol of spiritual and material abundance, the Ace of Pentacles can indicate good health, contentment, wealth, income, reward, money, and the material resources that free you to pursue and manifest your creativity, love, spirituality, and ideals. What new opportunities and resources have come to you recently? What dreams or life goals does this abundance support you to achieve?

Reversed

Reversed, the Ace of Pentacles can indicate financial disappointment. You experience the prosperity of the upright meaning—but without the joy or lasting stability. Your gain is fleeting and unsatisfying. The reversed Ace of Pentacles can also reveal an unhealthy love of money, mismanagement, wastefulness, or inflexible financial expectation. How can you establish a healthier relationship to money?

Symbolism

GARDEN Refuge, rest and reflection, simplicity, and abundance

GARDEN WALL Safety and protection

PENTACLE Earth and the body

MOUNTAIN PEAKS Ambition

TWO OF PENTACLES

NUMBER 2 Duality, Balance, Choice, Partnership

ASTROLOGY Jupiter in Capricorn

KEYWORDS Juggling, Balancing

In the Two of Pentacles, the figure juggles two pentacles representative of two different areas of your life. This card is about work-life balance, juggling the various elements of your life or leading a double life, such as working two very different jobs or having two lovers. The dynamic nature of your life gives you energy and keeps you interested.

Twos are also cards of choice. You might be making a decision about how you spend your time and manage your money. You are able to prioritize balance and harmony at this time.

ACE OF PENTACLES

TWO OF PENTACLES

THREE OF PENTACLES

Reversed

The reversed Two of Pentacles suggests that some things in your life have fallen out of balance, that you are drained and overwhelmed, or that the double life you are leading is not in integrity with your values or with the happiness of everyone involved. Is your work-life balance suffering? Are you having an affair? Be careful of assuming that you know what is best for everyone else involved. Whether you have caused or allowed this imbalance, or whether a person or situation in your life is demanding too much of your time and resources, find a way to restore balance.

Symbolism

TALL RED HAT Ability to hold many thoughts in one's head at once

SHIPS Commerce, wealth

WAVES Activity

THREE OF PENTACLES

NUMBER 3 Synthesis, Creativity, Dynamic Balance

ASTROLOGY Mars in Capricorn

KEYWORDS Meaningful Work, Collaboration, Renown

The Three of Pentacles shows a stonemason at work in a cathedral, conferring with a monk and a bishop who hold the blueprint of the stonemason's work. The inspired stonemason shapes durable, worldly form and substance to align with spiritual visions and truths.

In your life, this archetype will likely manifest as a rewarding and lasting collaboration, project, or enterprise. You are ready to use your skills and talents to shine in public, collaborating with others in service of a larger aim. Any project indicated by the Three of Pentacles aligns body, mind, and spirit. The project is public, accessible, and achieves widespread approval and lasting effect. What meaningful project are you working on? Who are you working with to achieve an ambitious goal much larger than yourself?

Reversed

Reversed, the Three of Pentacles can point to tedium and mediocrity, particularly in matters of career, and/or exhaustion and burnout. Consider ways to turn this situation around.

Symbolism

WORKBENCH Elevated by artistry, channeling a consciousness greater than one's own

MONK Spirituality, lifelong vocation

BISHOP Mentorship

CATHEDRAL The temple of the body

STONEWORK A spiritual, public, accessible, and long-lasting project

FOUR OF PENTACLES

NUMBER 4 Material Achievement, Structure, Order

ASTROLOGY Sun in Capricorn

KEYWORDS Security, Miserliness

The Four of Pentacles shows a miser holding on tightly to their wealth. The miser's energy and attention go into pinning down money with their feet and balancing it on their head, rather than into meaningful projects or relationships. Holding on to what you have is therefore a theme of this card. Fours are cards of stability: you recognize the value of protecting your property and managing your money well. If you have gone through an experience of poverty or a time of irresponsible spending, it can be important to find grounding in your newfound economic stability.

However, whether you are holding on to your resources responsibly or out of greed, don't let yourself get stuck here. Belongings, money, time, and other resources are all meant to flow among people. Their use should also respect the living earth and not be needlessly extracted or hoarded.

Reversed

Reversed, the Four of Pentacles indicates either a real need to pinch pennies or an extremely miserly attitude. If you are unemployed or dealing with big, unforeseen expenses, conserve as much money as you can for the time being, and don't be wasteful or careless with what you have. If, on the other hand, it is possible for you to be more openhearted and generous at this time, sharing what you have will bring you happiness.

Symbolism

GRAY SKY AND GROUND Feelings of insecurity

CITY Urban concerns and material pleasures, rather than connection to one's family group or to the earth

COIN ON HEAD Thoughts burdened by money

FIVE OF PENTACLES

NUMBER 5 Change, Challenge, Uncertainty, Mediation

ASTROLOGY Mercury in Taurus

KEYWORDS Hardship, Community Resilience

The figures in the Five of Pentacles trudge barefoot through the snow, against the wind. One person is injured. They are dressed in rags and likely ill from the cold. Financial hardship, poverty, loss, and destitution are themes of this card. The difficulties of such a situation threaten illness and depression.

However, in contrast to the lonely miser of the Four of Pentacles, the figures in this card have banded together, sharing encouragement and any money or food they have. This card insists that while you may feel outcast from society at large due to grief, poverty, or loss of a home, you do not feel alone. You feel strongly connected with others in similar situations, and these people will likely be your friends for a long time to come.

As long as you continue to care for yourself and your community, circumstances will change and you will lift each other up. Maintaining hope and love in your heart, and walking a path of intuition or faith, will allow you to keep your eyes open to the opportunities that are right for you. Keep doing the best you can. The health and generosity of the Six of Pentacles will be within reach soon enough.

Reversed

The Five of Pentacles, reversed, denotes bouncing back from an illness or an emotional or financial loss. What did you do to help turn your fate around? Continue to be diligent about your health and money. Your recovery is in your own hands.

Symbolism

BELL AROUND NECK Isolation (associated with leprosy)

MONEY TREE IN STAINED-GLASS WINDOW Focus on survival; opportunities for gaining riches are out of sight or out of reach

SIX OF PENTACLES

NUMBER 6 Harmony, Integration, Passivity

ASTROLOGY Moon in Taurus

KEYWORDS Generosity, Social Justice

The meaning of the Six of Pentacles is generosity and charity. While an aristocrat handing out a few coins to beggars is not a true or lasting redistribution of wealth or power, the spirit of the card is interpreted here as social justice.

Either you have achieved a level of economic stability that allows you to be generous or you are a recipient of someone else's generosity. Sixes represent harmony and balance. If you receive money, use it to bring balance to your own or someone else's financial situation, rather than blowing the cash on something frivolous. This money has come to you from someone who cares about your well-being. If you are giving resources to those in need, this card encourages you to understand the situation well so that your impact is effective and positive.

While the Six of Pentacles sometimes represents an occasion of unfelt, token charity, the spirit of the card describes acts that bring about a true balance of resources among people, alongside measured uses of resources that are in harmony with the earth.

Reversed

The Six of Pentacles, reversed, suggests that you are taking someone's generosity for granted or that someone else is making light of your generosity. Take good care of your resources. Appreciate what you have, give thanks where it is due, and don't allow your belongings to be literally or figuratively stolen from you.

Symbolism

SCALES Fairness, balance

GRAY SKY AND GROUND Uncertainty, poverty

SEVEN OF PENTACLES

NUMBER 7 Spirituality, Tests

ASTROLOGY Saturn in Taurus

KEYWORDS Investment, Uncertainty, Patience

The Seven of Pentacles shows a farmer regarding their crops with some unease. They watch the plants as if willing them to grow.

The Seven of Pentacles suggests that you have invested a lot of time, energy, and resources in a project that is now in its middle stages of completion. You feel uncertain about whether the project will succeed or fail. You have come far enough that you will be extremely disappointed and at a loss if you fail. Luckily, the Seven of Pentacles assures you that as long as you continue to plug away toward your goal, your project will inevitably bear fruit.

This card teaches patience, reminding you that you ultimately can't get worse at something you are actively trying to improve at, and that investment of effort always yields a return of learning, even if what you learn is not what you expected to learn.

Reversed

The Seven of Pentacles, reversed, indicates that you may be refusing to look at your financial situation or you are avoiding a reality check about the progress of an important project. Whether you are procrastinating or in denial about the importance or consequences of the situation at hand, take a look at your situation. Assess its progress and note any warning signs or issues. Taking necessary actions or making adjustments will make everything easier.

Symbolism

MOUNTAINS Goals, aspirations

GRAY SKY Uncertainty

SIX OF PENTACLES

SEVEN OF PENTACLES

EIGHT OF PENTACLES

NUMBER 8 Navigation, Prosperity, Authority

ASTROLOGY Sun in Virgo

KEYWORDS Hard Work, Concentration, Education, Training

The Eight of Pentacles signifies hard work. The figure in the Eight of Pentacles is working with their nose to the grindstone, hammering out pentacles—literally, making money.

Like an artisan or an apprentice (if you are not actually an artisan or apprentice), you are focusing on the task at hand, trusting that in doing this work you are laying the groundwork for the future. Due to your work now, you will ultimately be able to make big moves and attain more stability and spaciousness in your life. You work skillfully, and you are working your way toward the ease and luxury of the Nine of Pentacles.

Reversed

The Eight of Pentacles, reversed, indicates that you are either working too hard or not working hard enough. You may feel that your work is not satisfying or the right fit for you. Your lack of passion for this career path makes your training or work seem to require unreasonable amounts of effort. Or it is possible that you are on the right path, but feel unwilling to put in the work required to achieve your goals. If you are sure that you are on the wrong career path or that you are not working on the right project, change your course.

Symbolism

WORKBENCH Artisanship, artistry

TREE TRUNK (ON WHICH PENTACLES ARE HUNG) Growth

DISCARDED COIN (BENEATH WORKBENCH) Perfectionism

RED Vitality

BLUE Clarity of purpose

BLACK WORK APRON Protection

NINE OF PENTACLES

NUMBER 9 Completion, Meditation, Achievement of Goals

ASTROLOGY Venus in Virgo

KEYWORDS Retirement, Prosperity, Comfort

The Nine of Pentacles indicates a time of life when you are able to live your ideal lifestyle. Often, this card denotes retirement, but it can be any situation in which you have enough prosperity and time to create your own schedule and enjoy leisure, and enough experience and self-knowledge to know what you need, how you want to spend your time, and how to live in accordance with your values. You are intelligent and successful, and you have the luxury of enjoying the fruits of your accomplishments, particularly through lifestyle and through improving, beautifying, or enjoying the comforts of your home.

The Nine of Pentacles suggest that you are able to enjoy time to yourself. This might follow a period—or lifetime—of hard work, such as the Eight of Pentacles that precedes this card. You may also be focusing on enjoying the places and activities you already love, rather than exploring new options.

Be sure to be clear with yourself about why your alone time is important to you. Are you cultivating peace and contentment within yourself and enjoying a well-deserved rest, or are you actually generally distrustful of people and avoiding interaction—particularly with those outside of your social strata who could challenge your worldviews? The potential challenge of this card is loneliness.

Reversed

Reversed, the Nine of Pentacles indicates that even though you live a life of relative luxury, you are lonely—maybe even depressed. You may have focused much of your life on your career and are now experiencing regret that you did not do more to cultivate your relationships. Remember that it is never too late to change the course of your life, fill your life with love, and develop meaningful relationships.

Symbolism

GARDEN Refuge, rest and relaxation, abundance

GARDEN WALL Safety and protection

SNAIL Home

GRAPES Fruits of labor

FALCON Leisure, refinement; trained bird represents a disciplined mind

CASTLE HOME Security

YELLOW SKY Consciousness, joy

TEN OF PENTACLES

NUMBER 10 Pinnacle (of Success or Difficulty), Beginnings and Endings

ASTROLOGY Mercury in Virgo

KEYWORDS Generations, Community Resources, Foundation

In the Ten of Pentacles, we see three generations of a happy family with their two pet dogs. They are safe and comfortable in their large, secure home. In this card, resources have accumulated over the generations, but the Ten of Pentacles can also indicate a community rich in the combined spiritual or material resources or skillsets brought to it by its members.

The Ten of Pentacles indicates that you are giving or receiving support within your community or that you are joining a community—

EIGHT OF PENTACLES

NINE OF PENTACLES

TEN OF PENTACLES

for example, through marriage into a new family, being accepted into an academic institution, or becoming part of any other multigenerational group.

The pentacles in this card's image are arranged in the shape of the Tree of Life, indicating that through family or community support, you have the foundation to achieve not only worldly but also spiritual ideals.

Reversed

Reversed, the Ten of Pentacles reveals imbalance, tension, or outright conflict among generations of a family or community, likely due to money, property, inheritance, legacy, or difference in values. It is likely the case, however, that your family is more spiritually and materially stable together than apart.

Symbolism

TOWER Security and protection; sexuality and procreation

PATRIARCH'S GRAPE VINE CLOAK Fruits of labor, King of Pentacles

GREYHOUNDS Aristocracy, nobility

SCALE (CARVED INTO COLUMN) Balance, harmony

TREE OF LIFE Foundational spiritual spheres and pathways

PAGE OF PENTACLES

ASTROLOGY Earth Signs—Taurus, Virgo, Capricorn

KEYWORDS Apprentice, Diligence, Awe, Good News about Money

The Page of Pentacles is an apprentice of some kind. They are learning a new skill, and they are awed and inspired by their task, as we can see in the expression of wonder on this Page's face. The Pages are young people or people who are young in spirit. The Page of Pentacles is young in their development of a particular skill, trade, or course of study. They are either receiving training to develop a talent or they are learning a trade.

The Page of Pentacles is diligent. So, deal in practicalities at this moment. Make sure the logistics of your life are running smoothly: bills paid, property well maintained, and schedule running smoothly. If the Page of Pentacles represents you, you are likely feeling optimistic about the prosperous career that will come from this period of training and settling the logistical details of your life.

When the Page of Pentacles appears as a messenger or message, rather than as a personality or influence, this Page indicates that you will receive good news related to money, career, or education.

Reversed

Reversed, the Page of Pentacles is less diligent and more materialistic or wasteful. Are you or others (such as your children) being irresponsible with your property or money? The reversed Page of Pentacles may bring unwelcome financial news or unhappy news about your property. Be prepared to channel the upright qualities of the Page of Pentacles to stay positive and put things back in order.

Symbolism

FIELDS Fertility, growth

MOUNTAINS Aspirations

RED Vitality

GREEN Learning

KNIGHT OF PENTACLES

ASTROLOGY Leo, Virgo

KEYWORDS Provider, Responsible, Constructing, Secure

After the Page of Pentacles gains some fluency in their trade or sphere of study, they graduate to become the Knight of Pentacles, a person with a strong sense of purpose in matters of work or responsibility, but who has yet to master their craft and become a Queen or King of Pentacles. This is a time of alternating success, trial and error. Overall, however, the long-term vision of the Knight of Pentacles is strong. The oak leaves adorning their helmet and the head of the horse remind us that just as the acorn holds the blueprint of the entire maple tree, the Knight of Pentacles is able to plant seeds of success with confidence and patience.

The Knight of Pentacles is building something. You or someone in your life is working industriously, either literally in a field like construction or property, or else in finance. If the Knight of Pentacles represents you, you are methodically improving your skills or knowledge, developing a project, finding or securing a home, or building your career or income.

As a person or a partner, the Knight of Pentacles promises to be a provider (they are a provider-in-the-making, as compared to the King of Pentacles, who has mastered money and material care). Their focus is on stability and security, and they plan everything out ahead of time. Be aware that this Knight's patience can lean toward inertia and stubbornness.

Reversed

The reversed Knight of Pentacles emphasizes the negative polarity of this Knight upright: inertia and stubbornness. The reversed Knight of Pentacles is too cynical and cautious to motivate themself to do much of anything. They might also be miserly with their money. While the upright Knight of Pentacles is a provider and protector, the reversed Knight of Pentacles

PAGE of PENTACLES.

KNIGHT of PENTACLES.

QUEEN of PENTACLES.

KING of PENTACLES.

QUEEN OF PENTACLES

KING OF PENTACLES

neglects to care for the people in their life, focusing instead on materialistic desires or, in some cases, letting their belongings, resources, and career fall into disregard.

Symbolism

OAK LEAVES Sturdy trees begin as seeds

BLACK HORSE Protection

YELLOW SKY Rationality

BURGUNDY Steady and understated strength and life force

QUEEN OF PENTACLES

ASTROLOGY Sagittarius, Capricorn

KEYWORDS Resourceful, Pragmatic, Generous

The Queen of Pentacles is resourceful and pragmatic. They are likely a businessperson, entrepreneur, homemaker, or work in any profession involving practical, hands-on, or financial skills. They like to use their wealth to invest in experiences of beauty and to support others through charity or philanthropy. The Queen of Pentacles has a knack for channeling resources to make everyone involved feel grounded and supported.

The Queen of Pentacles indicates that you are financially comfortable, generous, and practically minded—or that you receive support from someone who has these qualities. If you are the Queen of Pentacles, you find practical, loving ways to care for those around you. You put attention into the details of your home, making it a sanctuary for those who visit. At an extreme, the Queen of Pentacles prizes orderliness over creativity or unconditional love.

Reversed

Reversed, the Queen of Pentacles is no longer the benefactor, but the dependent. They might neglect or mismanage their resources, or even find themself in debt. Alternately, the reversed Queen of Pentacles can go overboard in fulfilling their role—caring for everyone but themself. If you are feeling neglected or are resenting those you care for, step back and ask yourself whether you have taken responsibility for your own care. Keep in mind that you offer the best, most loving care when you are healthy and grounded.

Symbolism

RABBIT, FLOWER BLOSSOMS Springtime, fertility, luck

PEARS Fertility

STONE GOAT HEAD Hardworking and practical Capricorn; the god Pan (earthy sensuality)

YELLOW SKY Rationality

MOUNTAINS Aspiration

KING OF PENTACLES

ASTROLOGY Aries, Taurus

KEYWORDS Provider, Established, Security

The King and Queen of Pentacles are similar in many ways. They both work with the land, money, or property, and they both are generous with their time and material resources. The main difference lies in the King's emphasis on security and using their resource management skills to provide and to keep everyone safe, while the Queen offers more support than protection. The Queen's actions are more personalized (they are gardeners), while the King's actions are more systematized (they often manage agriculture).

The King of Pentacles is an expert in managing resources, including money and time. This King channels their deftness at management into being a provider for their family.

While the King of Pentacles finds much meaning in their role of keeping their family secure and safe, an unbalanced King of Pentacles acts overly protective of their property, boundaries, and family.

Reversed

The reversed King of Pentacles has lost sight of the purpose in managing resources so well. Instead of providing for their family and community, they set their morals aside in the pursuit of more wealth for themself. In their fixation on material gain and showiness, they may instigate corruption or gamble with unwise investments and actually go deep into debt.

Symbolism

GRAPES AND VINES Fruit of labor, abundance

BULLS' HEADS Aries

RIGHT FOOT ON BOAR'S HEAD Restraint of animal instincts

ARMOR Warrior

FLEURS-DE-LIS ON CROWN Ancient Egyptian fertility symbols

BLACK ROBE Protection

CASTLE Stronghold, security

SCEPTER WITH GLOBE Sovereignty in earthly plane

LAUREL WREATH Victory, power

8

THE MINOR ARCANA: SWORDS

SWORDS REPRESENT THE REALM OF MIND, thought, and the intellect. Both the sword and the mind are tools used for fighting for control. This suit represents incisive thought and critical-thinking skills, as well as actual conflicts with people in your life. The characteristics of Swords include aggressiveness, pain, and anxiety, but also rationality, clarity, and objectivity. Swords rule communication, ideologies, and paradigms. The element associated with Swords is air.

ACE OF SWORDS

NUMBER 1 Oneness, Beginnings, Power

ASTROLOGY Air Signs—Gemini, Libra, Aquarius

KEYWORDS Intellect, Success, Decisions

The Ace of Swords represents the unbounded power of the intellect. You are being presented with opportunities that will allow you to channel your intellectual energy into a great outcome.

An opportunity has come to you or is on its way in writing, publishing, or a field that involves mental acuity. This opportunity promises success, a feeling of victory, and the chance to become a leader in your field. The decisions you make and act upon now will bring improvements to your life and to your state of mind. Believe in the potential you sense in the air around you.

Reversed

Reversed, the positive assertiveness of the Ace of Swords turns into conflict and destructive uses of power. Watch out for your urge to fight or cut down someone who aggravates you. Listen to your conscience and let your heart guide you.

Symbolism

CROWN Divine power

LAUREL GARLAND Victory

RED BUD GARLAND Wisdom

MOUNTAINS Aspirations

TWO OF SWORDS

NUMBER 2 Duality, Balance, Choice, Partnership

ASTROLOGY Moon in Libra

KEYWORDS Indecision, Irresolution, Intuition

The Two of Swords represents indecision or a stalemate. You are faced with a choice that is hard because either option brings pain. The blindfold represents an inability to weigh options using sight or the rational mind. The night sky and moon indicate that you must go inward for your answers.

Wait. Be patient and let the answers reveal themselves to you, either through your intuition or in your outer life. You might have to let things remain unresolved a while longer.

Reversed

The Two of Swords, reversed, indicates poor judgment and making the wrong choice. You have chosen sides, rather than opting for a

ACE OF SWORDS

TWO OF SWORDS

THREE OF SWORDS

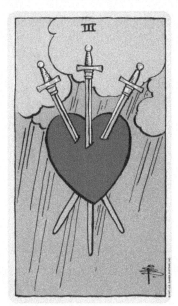

FOUR OF SWORDS

FIVE OF SWORDS

resolution. A rational decision or solution is possible, but you have decided against it. Alternately, the Two of Swords, reversed, can indicate making up your mind following a period of indecision. In partnerships, the reversed Two of Swords can suggest manipulation, deception, and even a fundamental incompatibility.

Symbolism

WAXING CRESCENT Growth, new beginnings, starting fresh

ROCKY WATERS Upset emotions

BLINDFOLD No answers for this situation can be attained using the rational mind

NIGHT SKY, MOON Intuition

THREE OF SWORDS

NUMBER 3 Synthesis, Creativity, Dynamic Balance

ASTROLOGY Saturn in Libra

KEYWORDS Sadness, Heartbreak, Catharsis

The Three of Swords is a card of sadness and hurt. Perhaps you've suffered a heartbreak. Your wound has been caused by issues related to the suit of Swords: communication, ideologies, intellectual paradigms, competitiveness, or aggression. You may have been attacked, or have recently confronted painful truths.

The pouring rain in this card shows that you are at least able to express this pain. Expression of the pain brings relief, catharsis, and the connection with loved ones that grief can offer. The Three of Swords encourages you not to bottle up your emotions, but to express them in order to let them go. This card assures you that releasing your emotions will give you the strength and clarity necessary to rise above your situation.

Reversed

As in the upright position, the Three of Swords, reversed, signifies loss and pain. However, this pain is muted or less extreme than in the upright Three of Swords. The pain described here might be caused by the extremes of the Swords traits: overthinking, abstracting, or compartmentalizing.

Symbolism

GRAY SKY Upsets

RAIN Catharsis, relief, purification

FOUR OF SWORDS

NUMBER 4 Material Achievement, Structure, Order

ASTROLOGY Jupiter in Libra

KEYWORDS Recovering, Rest, Reflection

In medieval Europe, it wasn't uncommon for a knight to have a coffin built for himself before he went to battle. If he came back alive, he would actually visit his own coffin and spend time lying in it. The purpose in doing this was to meditate on life, death, and the chances of fate. We see this pictured in the Four of Swords. Like the knight in the coffin, this card indicates that you are likely grappling with existential issues.

The Four of Swords represents the need to recover from a wounding (such as the heartbreak of the previous card, the Three of Swords), accident, or illness. It is possible that you got hurt while fighting for your convictions or doing something you love. This is a time of rest and recovery. Try not to waste energy fighting your need to rest. Allow yourself time to heal.

Reversed

The reversed Four of Swords indicates that you require a lot of rest or a long recovery. You may need to take time off work and come to terms with spending more time resting. If a respite is unavailable to you (likely due to your extensive responsibilities to loved ones), seek answers and fortitude through faith and spirituality.

Symbolism

COFFIN Mortality, rest

STAINED-GLASS WINDOW Depicts family and home; reminiscent of a holy place

FIVE OF SWORDS

NUMBER 5 Change, Challenge, Uncertainty, Mediation

ASTROLOGY Venus in Aquarius

KEYWORDS Conflict, Failure, Defeat

The Five of Swords signifies conflict, bad sportsmanship, and unfair advantages. Usually this card is interpreted to mean failure, such as losing a fight with a family member or struggling against an unfair boss or system—but the Five of Swords can also be interpreted to mean that you are the one doing the oppressing or being overly competitive.

In this card, the winner of the swordfight looks back smugly at the two people he has defeated. One person buries their head in their hands; the other walks away in dejection. The Five of Swords indicates spiteful winners and sore losers. Underlying the situation is a harsh dichotomy of failure and success that drives the losing party to succumb to dejection and the winner to gloat and be self-congratulatory. This frame of mind ignores the realities of our interconnectedness and inhibits the exploration, vulnerability, and sense of play that is necessary for us to learn and grow. The situation of this card exudes unfairness and a harshness that undercuts connection and creativity.

Reversed

The reversed Five of Swords emphasizes the unfairness of the fight at hand. It can indicate being on either side of a case of bullying or oppression. Either way, find constructive ways to deal with your anger or disappointment. If you have the upper advantage, don't gloat or continue to fight. If you have found yourself caught in the middle of an ego-driven fight that doesn't pertain to you, find a way to move on from the situation.

Symbolism

GRAY, JAGGED CLOUDS Rupture

RED Vitality

GREEN Lack of experience

CHOPPY WATER Unsettled emotions

SIX OF SWORDS

NUMBER 6 Harmony, Integration, Passivity

ASTROLOGY Mercury in Aquarius

KEYWORDS Travel, Perspective, Moving On

The Six of Swords signifies stepping back from your daily life, likely through travel, but possibly by simply taking time off or moving on from sorrow or a difficult relationship. This time of travel or moving on brings you out of a relatively narrow focus on the minutia of your life and offers you the perspective that only distance can bring. Your new perspective brings you peace and harmony. It also sparks reflection on what you value and the way you are living your life. This journey has a feeling of restfulness and spirituality.

This card shows an adult figure and child being ferried across a body of water. The water ripples on one side of the boat only, reflecting your position of having a calm or peaceful perspective on the daily tumults of your life, since you are on a journey or vacation, or are sitting this one out.

Reversed

The reversed Six of Swords can indicate difficulty getting away or escaping from a difficult situation. You might feel entrenched and frustrated. The advice of the reversed Six of Swords is to reconsider whether the path you have been focusing on is the right direction to take and whether now is actually the time to leave. You might be needed at the moment, and your current situation might yet have more to teach you.

Symbolism

LIGHT GRAY SKY Neutrality

CALM WATER Placid mind

RIPPLED WATER Difficulty or sorrow

SEVEN OF SWORDS

NUMBER 7 Spirituality, Tests

ASTROLOGY Moon in Aquarius

KEYWORDS Sneaking, Calculating, Stealing

The Seven of Swords shows a figure sneaking off with a bundle of swords. This person is clever, intelligent, and elusive. This is someone who uses their intellectual understanding of the situation and of the dynamics and personalities involved to get away with what they want. Depending on the situation, this person might be tactfully or selfishly avoiding confrontation, they might be outsmarting authorities to free themself from an oppressive situation, or they might be lying, evading, or stealing.

Look closely at the methods you are using to get what you want. Are you acting in good conscience? Why are you afraid of getting found out?

A more abstract, but interesting, meaning of this card is that you are sneaking away from norms or from your own inner critic in order to be more authentic or creative.

Reversed

The Seven of Swords, reversed, indicates that you are doing something unethical. Reconsider your options. Reversal can also signify that you are dealing with dishonest, untrustworthy people. Be sure to check the facts and ask for accountability.

Symbolism

TENTS Transience, impermanence

YELLOW Consciousness, sneaking away in broad daylight

EIGHT OF SWORDS

NUMBER 8 Navigation, Prosperity, Authority

ASTROLOGY Jupiter in Gemini

KEYWORDS Paralysis, Constraint, Ostracism

The Eight of Swords indicates paralysis. Like the blindfolded, bound figure in this card, you might feel trapped by too many options (represented by the eight swords stuck in the mud), all of which appear to be time sucks or nonsensical situations. You may feel unsupported and unable to differentiate between paths, either due to stress and overthinking, or to a situation in which other people seem to be in control of your fate, aware of aspects of your situation that you don't know about.

If you are in a situation described by the Eight of Swords, you may feel so cornered that your only way out is to channel creativity and love to transcend the paradigm you are stuck in.

Great inventions, social movements, and works of art are often created out of the catalyst of a dire situation.

Reversed

The reversal of the Eight of Swords exacerbates the upright meaning. Either you find yourself extremely incapacitated, or your mental indecision or isolation echoes through your emotions as shame, guilt, or regret. Again, channel your creativity and love to find release. In some cases, however, the reversed Eight of Swords indicates a release from constraints.

Symbolism

SHALLOW WATER, PUDDLES Superficiality, being trapped on the surface or outside a situation

CASTLE IN THE DISTANCE Outcast from civilization

RED Vitality; restrained life force

NINE OF SWORDS

NUMBER 9 Completion, Meditation, Achievement of Goals

ASTROLOGY Mars in Gemini

KEYWORDS Anxiety, Panic, Insomnia

The Nine of Swords shows a figure immersed in anxiety, kept awake at night by worry. This card indicates panic, insomnia, and nightmares. Rather than being directly engaged in a dangerous situation, the person in this card may be experiencing post-traumatic stress or may be overwhelmed by fears about what could happen to them or to someone they love.

The suit of Swords carries abstract energy. Your fears, lack of information, or inability to intervene, amplified by aloneness, might be paralyzing at this time. Additionally, an inner struggle may be playing out within you. You may be dwelling on past failures, possibly to the extreme that you become blind to current issues in your life. What worries are keeping you up at night? Whatever the case may be, do everything you can to get grounded and feel connected.

Reversed

Reversed, the Nine of Swords assures you that you have already experienced the lowest point of mental anguish. The worst of this period is behind you. Overall, this time of anxiety will not have lasting negative effects on your life.

Symbolism

12 ZODIAC SYMBOLS ON QUILT Many worries in many realms of life

PURPLE MATTRESS Intuition (here, pushing away from the comfort of the mattress)

ROSES Passion, impassioned worries

SIX OF SWORDS

SEVEN OF SWORDS

EIGHT OF SWORDS

NINE OF SWORDS

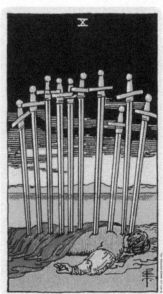

TEN OF SWORDS

TEN OF SWORDS

NUMBER 10 Pinnacle (of Success or Difficulty), Beginnings and Endings

ASTROLOGY Mercury in Virgo

KEYWORDS Betrayal, Backstabbing, Release

The figure in the Ten of Swords has been stabbed in the back. If this card represents you, someone has betrayed you or attacked you out of hatred, jealousy, or revenge. Likely, the retaliation committed against you was set off by your tendency to be a nonconformist. You have an important influence on those around you. Your way of being challenges people to reckon with themselves. The person or people who attacked or betrayed you didn't like what they found inside themselves and blamed you.

This is a horrible ordeal. But don't overlook the positive impact you have made in the world through following your convictions. Know that things can only improve from here. Trust that this trial is a period of removing yourself from this person's toxicity, and releasing them from your life. Rather than expecting situations like this to happen to you again, choose to let your resilience carry you forward.

Reversed

The Ten of Swords, reversed, indicates that you might be at least partly culpable for the terrible way things have gone. Or the reversal suggests that this situation might yet reveal more consequences. Still, it is never too late to start making amends or to take control of the direction of your life.

Symbolism

HAND GESTURE (BLESSING) Influence on society

BLACK SKY Oblivion

GLINT OF YELLOW SKY Glimmer of hope

FLOWING BLOOD Release, detox

PAGE OF SWORDS

ASTROLOGY Air Signs—Libra, Aquarius, Gemini

KEYWORDS Clever, Competitive, Minor Power Play, Useful Information or a Contract

The main quality of the Page of Swords is their ability to turn tense situations of challenge or conflict into opportunities. They are smart, witty, and strategic and communicate their ideas well. They are ambitious, though sometimes can be superficial.

The Page of Swords may refer to your own qualities or to the current influence in your life of a person with the qualities of the Page of Swords. Pages are beginners in learning the sphere of their suit. As the suit of Swords represents the mind, thought, and intellect, the Page of Swords is an intelligent young person (or a young person at heart) with a surprising ability to perceive the power dynamics of a given situation. This skill of theirs has not been refined, but sometimes that is what makes their perceptions so abrupt or shocking. The Page of Swords can err on the side of being judgmental or overconfident in their assessments.

Pages can also indicate messages that are on their way to you. As the suit of Swords represents the realm of the intellect, the Page of Swords is likely to bring useful information or a contract.

Reversed

Gossip rules the reversed Page of Swords. Either you are more worried about your reputation and fearful of social perceptions of your actions than you are focused on developing your own intellect, or you are spreading gossip about someone to tarnish their reputation and manipulate them. Don't allow gossipers, or the temptation of gossip, to shape the way you think. You are better than this.

Symbolism

STANDING ON A SMALL HILL Slightly competitive

WINDY DAY Instability

FLOCK OF BIRDS Group dynamics, air, thoughts

KNIGHT OF SWORDS

ASTROLOGY Taurus, Gemini

KEYWORDS Intelligent, Confrontation, Advocate

The Knight of Swords represents intellectual passion. At their best, they are advocates. They are the only Knight that seems to be engaged in battle. They signal confrontation and strong ideas. This Knight gets carried away by their ideas. They believe themself to be unstoppable, determined to pursue truth.

If the Knight of Swords faces another card, that card indicates the group, subject, or position the Knight is advocating for.

Reversed

The reversed Knight of Swords suggests that you or someone in your life is causing conflict and imbalance by shoving an idea down others' throats. Intellectual rigor has gone to the extreme of conflict for the sake of conflict, and this is causing rocky relationships and hasty communication in any area of your life. The reversed Knight of Swords can also signal excessive enthusiasm and getting carried away with ideas.

Symbolism

RIDING INTO THE WIND Confrontation

BUTTERFLIES Air, thoughts, metamorphosis of thought

HEART ON HORSE'S HALTER Knight wears his heart on his sleeve

BIRDS Air, higher thought

QUEEN OF SWORDS

ASTROLOGY Virgo, Libra

KEYWORDS Discerning, Independent, Intelligent, Boundaries

The Queen of Swords excels at critical thinking, discernment, and setting boundaries. They may be a software engineer, mathematician, politician or political theorist, lawyer, or anyone with a sharp mind and clear boundaries. They are likely in a position of authority and are highly principled.

The Queen of Swords indicates that you or someone in your life is independent, does not like to show weakness, and is incredibly intelligent. Behind the hard mask is someone who has been deeply hurt, but who has transformed the hurt into clear, safe boundaries, a keen understanding of power and instinct, and an incisive intelligence that is usually used to further a cause beyond themself.

Reversed

The reversed Queen of Swords feels wounded. They nurse their resentment, hold grudges, and always keep score. They can be elitist or pessimistic, and they hurt others in the ways they have been hurt. They are often close-minded, even cruel.

If this describes you, focus on establishing healthy boundaries so that you can both protect yourself and connect with others without setting yourself up for hurt. Be respectful of the boundaries of others. If, on the other hand, this describes someone in your life, establish clear boundaries with this person so that you do not allow them to hurt you.

Symbolism

WINGED CHERUB Protects the Garden of Eden

CUMULONIMBUS CLOUDS Thought, revelation

BLUE SKY Clear understanding

BUTTERFLIES Air, thoughts, metamorphosis of thought

BIRD Air, thought

PAGE OF SWORDS

KNIGHT OF SWORDS

QUEEN OF SWORDS

KING OF SWORDS

KING OF SWORDS

ASTROLOGY Capricorn, Aquarius

KEYWORDS Professional, Rational, Ambitious

The King of Swords brings order and discipline to everything they do. They are an authority figure who establishes strict rules and lays down the law. They are a doctor, academic, or other professional who holds a position of power.

At their best, the King of Swords enforces communally defined rules and standards of safety, justice, or intellectual rigor. They are logical, loyal, and clear-seeing. At their worst, however, they are authoritarian. The authoritarian King of Swords is unsympathetic, domineering, and cruelly calculating. In general, the King of Swords is ambitious, intellectual, charming, rationally minded, and has good judgment. They usually have a calm, balanced effect that makes the people around them feel reassured.

Reversed

Reversed, the ambition and authority of the King of Swords turns ruthless. They abuse their power relentlessly and see everything as a competition. If this describes someone in your life, unless you have a way to help this person restore their own compassion, it is likely best to get out of their way. If, on the other hand, you are the one who has gotten carried away with your own power, take a step down and a step back, and allow others to lead for a change. You will learn some worthwhile lessons.

Symbolism

FAIRY ON THRONE Titania, queen of the fairies

PURPLE CLOAK Intuition

BLUE ROBE Clarity

BUTTERFLIES Air, thoughts, developed thought

BIRDS Air, higher thought

THE MINOR ARCANA: WANDS

WANDS REPRESENT SPIRIT IN ACTION. They encompass the social, public, and creative realms where ideas are embodied and put into action. Wands show us our roles in family, community, and society. They illuminate our personalities and responsibilities. The qualities of Wands are enthusiasm, energy, and creativity. The element associated with Wands is fire.

ACE OF WANDS

NUMBER 1 Oneness, Beginnings, Power

ASTROLOGY Fire Signs—Aries, Leo, Sagittarius

KEYWORDS Creative Drive, New Projects

The Ace of Wands is like a magic wand. With clarity of vision and determination, you can use its energy to manifest something incredible. The Ace of Wands indicates the beginning of a new project or adventure. You feel inspired, energetic, and empowered. You feel sexy. You are driven by your creative instincts toward a new endeavor in your art, sex life, career, or community.

While the Ace of Wands represents real opportunity and the confidence necessary to succeed in your goals, it can also indicate being overeager. If that is the case, dial back your eagerness but move forward with your project or adventure.

Reversed

Ace of Wands, reversed, indicates setbacks or delays to beginning a new project or achieving goals, lack of willpower or vision, faltering conviction, creative blocks, or false starts. In relationships, it suggests cooled passions, time apart, lack of commitment, or difficulty conceiving. Readjust as needed.

Symbolism

EXUBERANT FOLIAGE New endeavors

RIGHT HAND Willpower

MOUNTAINS Aspirations

CASTLE Future attainments

TWO OF WANDS

NUMBER 2 Duality, Balance, Choice, Partnership

ASTROLOGY Mars in Aries

KEYWORDS Ambition, Plans, Success

In the Two of Wands, you begin to channel the ambitious energy of the Ace of Wands into actions and plans. You consider all the possible paths you could take, and you choose a way forward. This card indicates achievement and success in science, the arts, or another profession. You may have achieved or inherited great things or achieved early success in an endeavor, but your eye is on the horizon, looking toward even bigger accomplishments.

You are feeling visionary. Make an action plan to follow through on, but don't be hasty. How do you, or will you, find balance in your professional life and does this balance involve a creative partner? This card can also gesture to someone in your life who is worldly, intelligent, accomplished, and creative.

ACE OF WANDS

TWO OF WANDS

THREE OF WANDS

Reversed

Reversed, the Two of Wands indicates haste or inopportune timing in a new endeavor, initial success without follow-through, or misplaced trust in a romantic or professional partner, mentor, gatekeeper, or guide. There may be a feeling of having failed to surpass the achievements of a parent figure. Take time to reassess your plans and ambitions.

Symbolism

RED HAT Acting upon ideas of great achievement and influence; prosperity

GLOBE Planning for growth and expansion

FLOWERED CROSS The human body and blossoming consciousness; a harmony of power and justice

WAND SECURED TO THE FORTRESS WALL
Achievements already accomplished

WAND SURPASSING FIGURE'S HEIGHT
Aspiration and vision

WANDS Doorway of opportunity

THREE OF WANDS

NUMBER 3 Synthesis, Creativity, Dynamic Balance

ASTROLOGY Sun in Aries

KEYWORDS Project Launch, Productivity

The Three of Wands indicates success in putting ideas into action out in the world. The merchant watches their ships carry off goods to distant markets. This card takes place in the traditional world of commerce, business, and entrepreneurship, as well as in the contemporary world of activism, nonprofit work, and community-based projects.

After putting in great effort to overcome the challenges involved in turning an idea into action, you have launched your endeavor. Your idea has achieved a degree of workability, and you feel validated. You are able to look ahead and strategize. The Three of Wands indicates a situation in which your focus needs to be on both the big picture, and the daily minutia of the project. Don't lose perspective by either zooming too far out and overreaching the current scope of your project, or zooming too far in and failing to be strategic.

The way the merchant in this card holds one of the wands for support symbolizes the support they still need and receive from others. Stay strong in your vision, but be sure to value those who support you and to embrace cooperation!

Reversed

Reversed, the Three of Wands still carries the tidings of success that it does upright. However, amidst this success, you experience disappointments, setbacks, and delays due to competition in the field, carelessness, or lack of balance between action and planning. Communication problems and misunderstandings can also come up. You may doubt your project or yourself as a result of any of these issues, but the success you have achieved is still clear.

Symbolism

RED ROBES Ambition, action

GREEN ROBES Commerce

SHIPS IN THE DISTANCE Launched ideas, further opportunities on the horizon

MOUNTAINS Ambitions

FOUR OF WANDS

NUMBER 4 Material Achievement, Structure, Order

ASTROLOGY Venus in Aries

KEYWORDS Celebration, Security, Peace

The Four of Wands celebrates a literal or figurative harvest and the contributions of your closest in celebration. The chuppah, or wedding arch, features flowers and fruit of the harvest, denoting dedication come to fruition, often through harmonious, collaborative, community effort. Your community celebrates your individual and group achievements.

When you celebrate an event represented by the Four of Wands, as the figures in this card are pictured doing, you often celebrate a milestone in which your social position and title change, such as a graduation or marriage. You feel triumphant and joyous. The active, strategic, hardworking energy of the Three of Wands has paid off, and thanks to your efforts, you've reached a momentary plateau of stability, peace, and harmony. The emphasis in this card is the stability and peace that this achievement brings to your home life and community.

Reversed

Overall, the Four of Wands, reversed, carries the same meaning as upright. Sometimes, a reversal of this card indicates something or someone putting a damper on the party—perhaps you either overlook your blessings or don't feel worthy of them.

Symbolism

WEDDING ARCH/CANOPY Home and hospitality to one's guests

CASTLE Protection

YELLOW BACKGROUND Consciousness, joy, and manifestation

FIVE OF WANDS

NUMBER 5 Change, Challenge, Uncertainty, Mediation

ASTROLOGY Saturn in Leo

KEYWORDS Competition, Conflict, Chaos

After enjoying the stability and respite of the Four of Wands, it is time to mix things up a bit. Fives are dynamic; they throw a new element into the mix. The Five of Wands denotes a time that feels chaotic. You feel upset, confused, conflicted, fed up, or competitive.

The image in this card is deliberately unclear about whether the figures in the card are fighting, playing, building, or demolishing a structure. When many energies come together and start hashing it out, it is often impossible to understand the dynamics at first or predict the outcome. Therefore, this card can range from friendly competition and a needed dose of energy to outright fighting and unnecessary chaos or harm.

Often, this is a situation of healthy or constructive competition. Everyone in this competition likely stands a fair chance, so this can be an exciting time of testing and clarifying your intentions and plans. You might innovate or discover something about yourself that you otherwise would not have without this pressure and incentive. However, this card can also indicate infighting. Collaborators, family members, community members, or peers at school turn against each other, competing for a prize, status, or control.

Reversed

Reversed, the Five of Wands can indicate that you are ignoring or suppressing a conflict rather than dealing with it, expressing a volatile truth, or letting the situation play out. Alternatively, the Five of Wands, reversed, can carry the opposite meaning, suggesting resolution, reconciliation, and cooperation. The reversed Five of Wands may also show you rising out of a chaotic situation in which many things are fighting for your attention by choosing your priorities.

Symbolism

RED AND GREEN A clash of willpowers

CLEAR BLUE SKY A positive outcome is possible

SIX OF WANDS

NUMBER 6 Harmony, Integration, Passivity

ASTROLOGY Jupiter in Leo

KEYWORDS Victory, Validation, Messengers and Messages

The Six of Wands is the result of managing to survive the constructive competition and chaotic energy of the Five of Wands, pulling through with newfound competence and skills. In the uncertain environment of the Five of Wands, your talents were put to the test, your skills were refined through trial and error, and your fortitude was revealed. In that crucible, you created new ways of being in the world and interacting in your family, job, or wider community.

The Six of Wands shows a figure who has emerged victorious from a struggle or some kind of battle, or it can represent a messenger with incredible news. The Six of Wands can indicate a new level of mastery, one that is being vindicated or validated by those around you. This validation often comes in the form of a promotion. Your achievement or victory likely benefits many people and earns you wide support, respect, success and validation. Your efforts have paid off, and you can enjoy the benefits of success.

Reversed

Reversed, the Six of Wands can mean that a reward or promotion has been postponed, but will still arrive. It can also indicate being let down by someone.

Symbolism

LAUREL WREATHS ON HEAD AND WAND Victory, power, and widespread support and respect

GREEN GARMENT New life

TIGHT REIN Calm and skilled wielding of power and energy

SEVEN OF WANDS

NUMBER 7 Spirituality, Tests

ASTROLOGY Mars in Leo

KEYWORDS Courage, Self-Defense, Forcefulness, Stubbornness

The Seven of Wands shows a figure standing on literal high ground, using one wand to defend themselves against six attacking wands. In this fight-or-flight situation, the figure takes a strong stance and chooses to fight. This card signifies that you are defending or protecting yourself, your beliefs, and perhaps others against harassment or people who challenge your position.

FOUR OF WANDS

FIVE OF WANDS

SIX OF WANDS

SEVEN OF WANDS

The challenges are real, but they are absolutely surmountable as long as you don't let yourself get backed into a corner or wait too long to take action.

When the traits of this card become exaggerated, you can find yourself being overly defensive or sensitive to criticism. Ultimately, this card is about standing your ground. Whether out of stubbornness, fear, conviction in your beliefs, or a higher calling to protect something truly precious, you are protecting what matters to you.

Reversed

Seven of Wands, reversed, suggests that you are feeling reluctant, insecure, or indecisive, and these feelings are keeping you from defending yourself. You are not defenseless. Take a deep breath, and step up to this challenge.

Symbolism

STANDING ON HIGHER GROUND Moral high ground

BLUE SKY Clarity of conscience

GREEN Nature, growth

EIGHT OF WANDS

NUMBER 8 Navigation, Prosperity, Authority

ASTROLOGY Mercury in Sagittarius

KEYWORDS Movement, Acceleration, Communication

Movement and acceleration characterize the Eight of Wands. A project launch, relationship, or search for love is gaining momentum and reaching an apex of its trajectory. You know what you want and where you are aiming to land. You are ready, willing, and able to do all the tasks necessary to achieve success in your endeavor.

A card of communication, the Eight of Wands can signify the many communications involved in achieving your goal or that a message is on its way to you. The movement represented in these eight flying wands can signify rapid changes or transitions, and the need to do many things at once in an effort to keep up. Things feel lively and possibly up in the air. You might feel impatient to find out how things will land. The transition can also be from one place to another: you might be traveling.

Out of balance, the Eight of Wands indicates that you may be doing too many things at once—that there is little meaning in all this energy, and you feel needlessly frenetic and overstimulated.

Reversed

When the Eight of Wands is reversed, it suggests that you are running yourself into the ground with your ceaseless activity. You are not accomplishing what you intend to accomplish, you are refusing to prioritize, or you are experiencing burnout. Slow down. Alternately, the reversal shows your reluctance to take on the liveliness of this card. You are dragging your feet, procrastinating, and moving more slowly than is appropriate for the situation. Take action.

Symbolism

BLUE SKY Clarity

RIVER Flow

NINE OF WANDS

NUMBER 9 Completion, Meditation, Achievement of Goals

ASTROLOGY Moon in Sagittarius

KEYWORDS Guarding, Protecting, Defending

Guarding one's boundaries is the theme of the Nine of Wands. The figure in this card is eager to protect themselves and their achievements, despite already having been wounded in a fight, as we see from the bandage on their head. The Nine of Wands indicates that you truly believe you need to defend yourself from attack, despite your exhaustion from fighting and indications that you might be overreacting.

Compared to the Seven of Wands, in which you are driven by your ideals to defend yourself, the defensiveness of the Nine of Wands is almost defensiveness as a habit. This card does not show any oncoming attackers, but the figure nonetheless expects to be attacked. Ask yourself whether your vigilance serves a purpose right now. Are there challenges on the horizon that you need to be prepared for? If so, is defense, rather than resolution, the best way to prepare or is paranoia getting the best of you?

The Nine of Wands indicates that you or someone very present in your life right now is a tough, determined survivor who has fought their way to a strong position. This card pushes you to observe how you treat vulnerability in yourself and others, and encourages you to conserve your energy or take a gentler approach.

Reversed

Reversed, the Nine of Wands signifies that you feel discouraged and exhausted from fighting. No matter how much you fight, the unreasonable or demanding person or people in your life have not backed down. You are on the verge of giving in. Check in with yourself about whether you are being overly defensive or if your need to defend yourself is real. Either way, change your tactic.

EIGHT OF WANDS

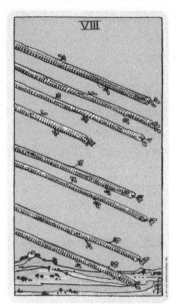

NINE OF WANDS

TEN OF WANDS

Symbolism

FENCE OF WANDS Responsibilities and achievements

STONE PLATFORM Solid foundation, sure footing

HEAD BANDAGE Past struggles

TEN OF WANDS

NUMBER 10 Pinnacle (of Success or Difficulty), Beginnings and Endings

ASTROLOGY Saturn in Sagittarius

KEYWORDS Responsibilities, Burdens, Strength

The Ten of Wands indicates that you are burdened with social, domestic, or career-related responsibilities. You have taken on a lot, perhaps too much. This card shows a figure who is more or less able to carry these responsibilities. Their back is bent under the weight of 10 wands, but they are strong enough to carry their burden at least a little further. The path ahead is clear, and the figure has almost made it home.

You are almost to the finish line, but without being able to see where you are going, for all that you carry, you might literally lose sight of your destination. The burden of wands is at least gathered together tightly, suggesting unity of purpose and vision. This card signifies an ending, a final push. With strength, persistence, and as much prioritizing and foresight as possible, you will be able to persevere through this moment and enjoy relief and reward on the other side.

If this card turns up in many of your readings, think about whether it is healthy for you to sustain so many burdens all the time and what you might be able to do to lighten the load.

Reversed

Reversed, the Ten of Wands represents sustained stress and an unwillingness to put your burden down. You may be working to keep everyone happy without knowing what you personally want or need. Take some time to prioritize, delegate, restore your health, and reconnect with your long-term goals.

Symbolism

BLUE SKY Things will clear up

FARMLAND Fertile ground, laboring toward the harvest

PAGE OF WANDS

ASTROLOGY Fire Signs—Aries, Leo, Sagittarius

KEYWORDS Inspired, Enthusiastic, Good News

The Page of Wands is inspired, confident, and energetic. They are young or young at heart and full of spirit. They love to create and go on adventures. They are earnest, and in their earnestness, they are trustworthy. The Page of Wands may refer to your own qualities or to the current influence in your life of a person with the qualities of the Page of Wands.

Pages are beginners in learning the sphere of their suit. As the suit of Wands represents the realm of social roles in family and community, as well as creative inspiration, the Page of Wands is an inspired and idealistic young person—or anyone young at heart or new to a community or sphere of influence—who has interest, curiosity, and questions about their own identity and role in the world.

Pages can also appear as messengers or messages. As the suit of Wands deals with communication, you will likely receive either good news or lots of phone calls or emails from family or work.

Reversed

Reversed, the Page of Wands indicates that this card's upright qualities are latent. Out of fear or boredom, your qualities of creativity, energy, and sense of adventure are blocked. The reversed Page of Wands can also indicate that you or someone influencing you is refusing to focus on work that needs to be done or relationships that need to be tended to, because they are too focused on satisfying their need for excitement.

Symbolism

SALAMANDERS ON TUNIC Spiritual rebirth

RED FEATHER Vitality, energy, aspiration

PYRAMIDS Inspiration from cultural, spiritual, and creative achievement

KNIGHT OF WANDS

ASTROLOGY Scorpio, Sagittarius

KEYWORDS Impassioned, Enthusiastic, Inspired `

The Knight of Wands may be the most impassioned card in the entire deck. This Knight oscillates between desire, inspiration, anger, and enthusiasm. Nothing, it seems, puts a damper on their enthusiasm. This card describes you or someone in your life who is habitually or currently ambitious, enthusiastic, or inspired.

The Knight of Wands indicates a time of energy and direction. Desire, sexuality, and fervent work on creative projects defines your days. If the Knight of Wands faces another card in a spread, the card it faces can indicate the object or realm where the Knight of Wands places their energy.

Reversed

Reversed, the Knight of Wands indicates that too much fire is fueling your personality or that of someone in your life. Someone is being competitive and egotistical. Try to help yourself or this person get back in touch with the purer qualities of the upright Knight of Wands: inspiration and creative enthusiasm. Alternatively, the reversed Knight of Wands can indicate that this Knight's upright qualities are blocked due to insecurity. Again, let your pure enthusiasm reinspire you and give you direction.

Symbolism

FLAMES OR RED FEATHERS Fire, passion, desire, energy, drive

PYRAMIDS Cultural, spiritual, and creative achievement

SALAMANDERS ON TUNIC Fire, spiritual resilience

QUEEN OF WANDS

ASTROLOGY Pisces, Aries

KEYWORDS Visionary, Entrepreneur, Self-Confident

The Queen of Wands is a driven creative visionary. Friendly, inspiring, and charismatic, the Queen of Wands creates large networks through which they receive, impart, and develop ideas. They are a confident, ambitious leader or entrepreneur. Their strong vision and innovation are inspiring, and their down-to-earth yet inspired energy is contagious.

The Queen of Wands points to these qualities in yourself or to the influence of a person in your life who embodies these qualities. If the qualities of the Queen of Wands are guiding your life right now, you are enjoying the working success of projects and the social networks that support them. You are a leader, a visionary, and someone who many people are glad to have as a mentor, colleague, collaborator, or friend.

Reversed

Reversed, the Queen of Wands is strong-willed and controlling. This card, reversed, might signal conflict with your mother or with a strong-willed person in your life. If this is the case, look to the positions of the cards, as well as the other cards in the spread, for insights into the nature of this conflict and how to address it.

PAGE OF WANDS

KNIGHT OF WANDS

PAGE of WANDS.

KNIGHT of WANDS.

QUEEN of WANDS.

KING of WANDS.

QUEEN OF WANDS

KING OF WANDS

If you are the one being bossy or strong-willed, reconnect with your creativity and inspiration and the control you have to create your own projects. Trust your own creative potential, and allow others to follow their own paths. You will likely find that the more luminous your own creative work, the more others will seek you out for advice and guidance.

Symbolism

SUNFLOWERS Growth, energy, vision

LIONS AND CATS Power, courage, leadership, magic, and Sekhmet (Egyptian deity of healing and warfare)

YELLOW Conscious awareness, joy, actualizing ideas

KING OF WANDS

ASTROLOGY Cancer, Leo

KEYWORDS Wise, Charismatic, Successful

The King of Wands is charismatic, worldly, wise, good at communicating, and passionate. They are a free spirit who has achieved mastery in their field and discipline in their passions. They like to talk, travel, and be in control. They are the Page or Knight of Wands grown up. They may be a spiritual elder, actor, or CEO.

The King of Wands takes risks, but they are so skilled in their field and so energetic that they catch issues before anything gets out of hand. The King of Wands either indicates these qualities in you, or the influence of this King's personality in your life.

If the qualities of the King of Wands describe your current situation, you are expressing mastery in your creativity and assurance in your relationships and roles.

Reversed

The reversed King of Wands is opinionated, impetuous, competitive, controlling, micromanaging, or even tyrannical. If this describes you currently, it is important to gain (or regain) mastery over your passions. Channel your anger and dive into practices of spiritual mastery, creative expression, or leadership. Wielding your passion in these ways will bring you more meaningful success and will prevent heartache for the many people affected by your power. If the reversed King of Wands is exerting their power over you, look to the positions of the cards, as well as the other cards in the spread, for insights into the nature of this issue and how to address it.

Symbolism

ORANGE AND RED Fire, spiritual strength, energy, vitality, ambition

SALAMANDERS Fire, spiritual strength and resilience

LIONS Power, courage, vitality, leadership

THE CHARIOT.

THE HIGH PRIESTESS.

THE SUN.

VIII

III

KNIGHT of CUPS.

III

ACE of PENT

II

VI
THE LOVERS.

IV

XVII
THE STAR.

VI

XI
JUSTIC

X

X

I

IV

XVI

CONCLUSION

I HOPE THIS BOOK HAS HELPED YOU use the tarot to connect with your own intuitive capabilities of self-discovery and growth. In addition to providing you with descriptions of the cards in both the Major and Minor Arcana, I have suggested a method for connecting with the cards in chapter 4. When you use the tarot to consistently access profound depths of meaning and tap into your insight to become truer to yourself, you can start living your life in alignment with possibilities beyond what you were previously able to imagine.

In this book, we covered the history and function of the cards as ordinary yet magical objects. While this spiritual tool was created as a simple card game and uses a patchwork of symbolism, it has the power to evoke our deepest truths, surprising us with its accuracy. This book's instructions for preparing your space for readings and caring for your deck indicate the importance of ritual, but emphasize your ability to create and personalize your practice.

As you proceed deeper into your tarot practice, take your study of the cards seriously, but allow trust to lead you. There are many tarot-reading skills you can only learn through actually reading the cards. So, trust yourself and the process, keeping in mind that you can only gain confidence in your abilities by first taking leaps of faith, like The Fool.

Trust what the tarot cards tell you. As tempting as it can be to only believe in the cards when they're telling us something nice, the unwelcome messages may end up being the ones you come to be most grateful for, the ones you learn the most from and that help you grow, freeing you from limitation. Finding and embracing trust will get easier as you continue to develop your connection with your cards, and this will lead you to feel more confidence in your life decisions and to shape your life more meaningfully. Trust, too, that trust will come.

Through your ability to perceive the connections between the abstract and the concrete, the potential and the actual, the cards and your life, and through your willingness to express your insights and use them to grow and to uplift everyone you meet, may you find freedom and unconditional love.

APPENDIX:
CARDS & KEYWORDS QUICK REFERENCE

Major Arcana Card Meanings

CARD	UPRIGHT KEYWORDS	REVERSED KEYWORDS
0. THE FOOL	Leap of Faith, Innocence, Adventure	Impulsive, Inhibited
I. THE MAGICIAN	Creativity, Manifestation, Ability	Abuse of Power, Powerlessness
II. THE HIGH PRIESTESS	Inner Knowledge, Intuition, Duality	Secrecy, Deception, Ignored Intuition
III. THE EMPRESS	Beauty, Motherhood, Creativity	Difficulties with Motherhood, Conflict with One's Mother, Creative Blocks
IV. THE EMPEROR	Reliability, Fatherhood, Responsibility	Unreliability, Coup, Revolution
V. THE HIEROPHANT	Education, Knowledge, Religion, Conformity	Poor Leadership or Free-Spirited Visionary
VI. THE LOVERS	Connection, Fulfillment, Love, Choice	Temptation, Indecision, Betrayal
VII. THE CHARIOT	Momentum, Breakthrough, Travel	Loss of Control, Disappointments
VIII. STRENGTH	Compassion, Perseverance, Power	Forceful, Passive
IX. THE HERMIT	Wisdom, Seeker, Inner Voice	Closed Off
X. WHEEL OF FORTUNE	Change, Patterns, Fortune	Standstill, Closure, Resisting Fate
XI. JUSTICE	Balance, Objectivity, Fairness, Equity	Injustice

Major Arcana Card Meanings *continued*

CARD	UPRIGHT KEYWORDS	REVERSED KEYWORDS
XII. THE HANGED MAN	Trust, Self-Sacrifice, Waiting	Despair, Loss of Faith, Undue Self-Sacrifice
XIII. DEATH	Endings, Transformation, Grief, Rebirth	Fear, Confusion, Resisting Transformation
XIV. TEMPERANCE	Creativity, Art, Healing, Balance	Imbalance, Indulgence, Deprivation
XV. THE DEVIL	Vitality, Play, Temptation, Oppression	Release, Severance
XVI. THE TOWER	Destruction, Consequences, Catastrophe, Detoxification	Caught in the Crossfire
XVII. THE STAR	Guiding Vision, Healing, Creativity	Naïveté, Obliviousness, Cynicism
XVIII. THE MOON	Dreams, Instinct, Crisis	Trauma, Emotional Buildup, Caught in Old Patterns
XIX. THE SUN	Joy, Success, Health, Children	Same as Upright, or Loss of Something Cherished
XX. JUDGEMENT	Higher Calling, Criticism, Judgment Call, Absolution	Overly Critical
XXI. THE WORLD	Completion, Celebration, Wholeness	Working within Limitations

Minor Arcana Card Meanings: Cups

CARD	UPRIGHT KEYWORDS	REVERSED KEYWORDS
ACE OF CUPS	Love, Joy, Spirituality	Spiritual Egotism, Creative or Emotional Blocks
TWO OF CUPS	Partnership, Friendship, Cooperation	Miscommunication, Codependency
THREE OF CUPS	Celebration, Friendship, Camaraderie	Overreliance on Friends, Seeking Approval, Premature Celebration
FOUR OF CUPS	Rest, Reflection, Boredom, Apathy	Reengagement or Dissatisfaction
FIVE OF CUPS	Grief, Sorrow, Mourning	Overwhelming Loss or Recovering from Grief, Getting Support
SIX OF CUPS	Childhood Comforts, Nostalgia	Nostalgia or Unhappy Childhood Memories
SEVEN OF CUPS	Fantasy, Creativity, Temptation	Delusion, Fantasy, or Resisting Temptation
EIGHT OF CUPS	Leaving, Wandering, Seeking	Drifting, Lack of Patience, or Returning Home
NINE OF CUPS	Hosting, Welcoming, Enjoyment	Undeserving of Enjoyment, Overindulgence
TEN OF CUPS	Family Love, Togetherness, Joy	Family Love, Threat to Harmony, Distracted by Ideals
PAGE OF CUPS	Innocent, Imaginative, Dreamer, Inspiring News	Naïve, Irresponsible, Impulsive
KNIGHT OF CUPS	Romance, Idealism, Passion, Inspiration	Spiritual Blocks, Rejection, Possessiveness in a Relationship
QUEEN OF CUPS	Nurturing, Healing	Depression, Victimhood, Draining
KING OF CUPS	Calm, Shoulder to Cry On	Insecurity, Shame, Hatred, Betrayal

Minor Arcana Card Meanings: Pentacles

CARD	UPRIGHT KEYWORDS	REVERSED KEYWORDS
ACE OF PENTACLES	Perfection, Contentment, Prosperity	Financial Disappointment, Materialism, Wastefulness
TWO OF PENTACLES	Juggling, Balancing	Work-Life Imbalance, Drained, Overwhelmed
THREE OF PENTACLES	Meaningful Work, Collaboration, Renown	Tedium, Mediocrity, or Burnout
FOUR OF PENTACLES	Security, Miserliness	Financial Need or Miserliness
FIVE OF PENTACLES	Hardship, Community Resilience	Physical or Financial Recovery
SIX OF PENTACLES	Generosity, Social Justice	Generosity Taken for Granted
SEVEN OF PENTACLES	Investment, Uncertainty, Patience	Avoiding Responsibility
EIGHT OF PENTACLES	Hard Work, Concentration, Education, Training	Overwork, Unsatisfying Career
NINE OF PENTACLES	Retirement, Prosperity, Comfort	Loneliness, Regretful
TEN OF PENTACLES	Generations, Community Resources, Foundation	Family Conflict over Finances, Property, or Values
PAGE OF PENTACLES	Apprentice, Diligence, Awe, Good News about Money	Materialistic, Wasteful, Unhappy News about Property or Finances
KNIGHT OF PENTACLES	Provider, Responsible, Constructing, Secure	Inertia, Stubbornness, Cynical, Neglectful
QUEEN OF PENTACLES	Resourceful, Pragmatic, Generous	Dependent, Mismanaging
KING OF PENTACLES	Provider, Established, Security	Greed, Materialism, Corruption, Gambling

Minor Arcana Card Meanings: Swords

CARD	UPRIGHT KEYWORDS	REVERSED KEYWORDS
ACE OF SWORDS	Intellect, Success, Decisions	Conflict, Abuse of Power
TWO OF SWORDS	Indecision, Irresolution, Intuition	Poor Judgment, Choosing Sides, or Newfound Clarity
THREE OF SWORDS	Sadness, Heartbreak, Catharsis	Mitigated Pain
FOUR OF SWORDS	Recovering, Rest, Reflection	Long Recovery
FIVE OF SWORDS	Conflict, Failure, Defeat	Unfair Fight, Bullying, Oppression
SIX OF SWORDS	Travel, Perspective, Moving On	Stuck in a Rut
SEVEN OF SWORDS	Sneaking, Calculating, Stealing	Dishonesty, Untrustworthiness
EIGHT OF SWORDS	Paralysis, Constraint, Ostracism	Paralyzing Indecision or Release
NINE OF SWORDS	Anxiety, Panic, Insomnia	Pulling Through
TEN OF SWORDS	Betrayal, Backstabbing, Release	Culpability, More Crisis to Come
PAGE OF SWORDS	Clever, Competitive, Minor Power Play, Useful Information or a Contract	Gossip, Tarnished Reputation, Manipulation
KNIGHT OF SWORDS	Intelligent, Confrontation, Advocate	Conflict, Carried Away
QUEEN OF SWORDS	Discerning, Independent, Intelligent, Boundaries	Resentment, Spiteful
KING OF SWORDS	Professional, Rational, Ambitious	Ruthlessness, Abuse of Power, Overly Competitive

Minor Arcana Card Meanings: Wands

CARD	UPRIGHT KEYWORDS	REVERSED KEYWORDS
ACE OF WANDS	Creative Drive, New Projects	Delays, Lack of Willpower, Cooled Passions
TWO OF WANDS	Ambition, Plans, Success	Bad Timing, No Follow-Through
THREE OF WANDS	Project Launch, Productivity	Delays Amidst Success, Mild Disappointments, Communication Problems
FOUR OF WANDS	Celebration, Security, Peace	Same as Upright, or Dampened or Ignored Celebration
FIVE OF WANDS	Competition, Conflict, Chaos	Ignoring or Suppressing Conflict, or Cooperation or Prioritizing
SIX OF WANDS	Victory, Validation, Messengers and Messages	Postponed Promotion, Letdown
SEVEN OF WANDS	Courage, Self-Defense, Forcefulness, Stubbornness	Conflict-Avoidant
EIGHT OF WANDS	Movement, Acceleration, Communication	Senseless Activity or Procrastination
NINE OF WANDS	Guarding, Protecting, Defending	Exhausting Fight, Giving In
TEN OF WANDS	Responsibilities, Burdens, Strength	Stress, Inability to Prioritize
PAGE OF WANDS	Inspired, Enthusiastic, Good News	Blocked Energy or Overindulgence in Excitement
KNIGHT OF WANDS	Impassioned, Enthusiastic, Inspired	Competitive, Egotistical, Insecure
QUEEN OF WANDS	Visionary, Entrepreneur, Self-Confident	Controlling, Conflict with Someone Controlling
KING OF WANDS	Wise, Charismatic, Successful	Opinionated, Impetuous, Competitive, Micromanaging, Tyrannical

RESOURCES

RWS-BASED TAROT DECKS

Next World Tarot by Cristy C. Road—a socially engaged and wonderfully imagined tarot deck (also available in Spanish as *El Tarot Del Próximo Mundo*)

Osho Zen Tarot by Osho—a Zen-inspired tarot deck

Rider-Waite-Smith Tarot by Arthur Edward Waite and Pamela Colman Smith—the standard tarot deck used in this book (also called the Rider Deck and Rider-Waite Deck)

Sakki-Sakki Tarot by Monicka Clio Sakki—a tarot deck that features creative, brightly colored imagery; includes one extra Major Arcana card: The Artist

Slow Holler Tarot by Slow Holler Collective—an enchanting, collectively drawn tarot deck by queer and Southern artists

Tarot of the Dead by Monica Knighton—a tarot deck inspired by *Día de los Muertos* (The Day of the Dead, a traditional holiday in Mexico, celebrated by Mexicans around the world)

Wild Unknown Tarot by Kim Krans—an evocative, animal-themed tarot deck

HELPFUL WEBSITES

Crystal Clear Reflections: Tarot Divinations
Crystal-reflections.com/tarot3

Little Red Tarot: An Alternative Approach to Tarot (Beth Maiden, Founder)
Littleredtarot.com

HELPFUL BOOKS

Pollack, Rachel. *The Complete Illustrated Guide to Tarot.* New York, NY: Gramercy Books, 2004.

Pollack, Rachel. *Seventy-Eight Degrees of Wisdom: A Book of Tarot.* London, UK: Thorsons, 1997.

Renee, Janina. *Tarot: Your Everyday Guide.* St. Paul, MN: Llewellyn Publications, 2000.

Warwick-Smith, Kate. *The Tarot Court Cards: Archetypal Patterns of Relationship in the Minor Arcana.* Rochester, VT: Destiny Books, 2003.

REFERENCES

Dean, Liz. *The Ultimate Guide to Tarot: A Beginner's Guide to the Cards, Spreads, and Revealing the Mystery of the Tarot.* Beverly, MA: Fair Winds Press, 2015.

Eason, Cassandra. *Complete Guide to Tarot.* Freedom, CA: The Crossing Press, 1999.

Greer, Mary K. *Tarot for Your Self: A Workbook for Personal Transformation.* Franklin Lakes, NJ: New Page Books, 2002.

Greer, Mary K. *21 Ways to Read a Tarot Card.* St. Paul, MN: Llewellyn Publications, 2006.

Greer, Mary K. "The Visconti Tarots." Mary K. Greer's Tarot Blog. July 3, 2011. Accessed December 24, 2017. https://marykgreer.com/2011/07/03/the -visconti-tarots.

Huson, Paul. *Mystical Origins of the Tarot: From Ancient Roots to Modern Usage.* Rochester, VT: Destiny Books, 2003.

Nichols, Sallie. *Jung and Tarot: An Archetypal Journey.* San Francisco, CA: Red Wheel/Weiser, 1980.

Norfleet, Phil. "Alfred Stieglitz and Pamela Colman Smith." Accessed November 20, 2017. http://pcs2051.tripod.com/stieglitz_archive.htm#.

Pollack, Rachel. *The Complete Illustrated Guide to Tarot.* New York, NY: Barnes and Noble Books, 1999.

Quinn, Paul. *Tarot for Life: Reading the Cards for Everyday Guidance and Growth.* Wheaton, IL: Theosophical Publishing House, 2009.

Warwick-Smith, Kate. *The Tarot Court Cards: Archetypal Patterns of Relationship in the Minor Arcana.* Rochester, VT: Destiny Books, 2003.

Wen, Benebell. *Holistic Tarot: An Integrative Approach to Using Tarot for Personal Growth.* Berkeley, CA: North Atlantic Books, 2015.

INDEX

A

Ace of Cups, 117, 118
Ace of Pentacles, 133, 134
Ace of Swords, 149, 150
Ace of Wands, 163, 164
Action, 67–68
Alchemy, 15, 18–19
Altars, 13
Archetypes, 3, 9. *See also* Symbolism
Astrology, 15, 18

B

Best practices, 8

C

Celtic Cross spread, 45–49
Chariot, The, 86–87
Christianity, 14
Comparing Your Options spread, 54–57
Conscious awareness, 65–67
Court de Gébelin, Antoine, 4
Creative expression, 66–67
Crowley, Aleister, 6
Cups, 22, 116
  card meanings, 182
  Ace of Cups, 117, 118
  Two of Cups, 117–119
  Three of Cups, 118, 119–120
  Four of Cups, 120, 123
  Five of Cups, 120–121, 123
  Six of Cups, 121–122, 123
  Seven of Cups, 122–124
  Eight of Cups, 124, 126
  Nine of Cups, 124–125, 126
  Ten of Cups, 125–127
  Page of Cups, 127–128, 130
  Knight of Cups, 128–129, 130
  Queen of Cups, 129–131
  King of Cups, 130, 131
Curtis, Alia, 65

D

Death, 98–99
Decks
  attuning, 12
  caring for, 12
  cleansing, 12
  purifying, 11–12
  Rider-Waite-Smith, 4, 5–6, 11, 14
  selecting, 11
  shuffling, 16–17
  Visconti-Sforza, 3–4, 19
Devil, The, 102–103
Divination, 3, 4, 6–7

E

Egyptian mythology, 15
Eight of Cups, 124, 126
Eight of Pentacles, 140, 142
Eight of Swords, 154–155, 156
Eight of Wands, 170–171, 172
Emperor, The, 80–81
Empress, The, 78–79
Essential Keys spread, 42–44

F

Five of Cups, 120–121, 123
Five of Pentacles, 136–137, 139
Five of Swords, 150, 152–153
Five of Wands, 167, 169

Fool, The, 72–73
Fool's Journey, 20, 70
Four of Cups, 120, 123
Four of Pentacles, 136, 139
Four of Swords, 150, 151–152
Four of Wands, 23, 166, 169

G

Greek mythology, 15
Greer, Mary K., 50, 64

H

Hanged Man, The, 96–97
Hermetic Order of the Golden Dawn, 4, 18–19
Hermit, The, 90–91
Hierophant, The, 82–83
High Priestess, The, 76–77
Huson, Paul, 3

I

Inner experience, 64–65
Insight, 65–68
Intuition, 8, 64–68

J

Judgement, 112–113
Jung, Carl, 3, 9
Justice, 94–95

K

Kabbalah, 4, 15, 18–19
King of Cups, 130, 131
King of Pentacles, 145, 147
King of Swords, 160–161
King of Wands, 176, 177
Kings, 23
Knight of Cups, 128–129, 130
Knight of Pentacles, 144–146

Knight of Swords, 158–159, 160
Knight of Wands, 174–175, 176
Knights, 23

L

Layouts. See Spreads
Let Go/Grow spread, 34–35
Lévi, Éliphas, 4, 18
Life Path spread, 38–41
Lovers, The, 84–85

M

Magic (magick), 6–7
Magician, The, 74–75
Major Arcana, 3, 20–21, 70–71
    card meanings, 180–181
    Chariot, The, 86–87
    Death, 98–99
    Devil, The, 102–103
    Emperor, The, 80–81
    Empress, The, 78–79
    Fool, The, 72–73
    Hanged Man, The, 96–97
    Hermit, The, 90–91
    Hierophant, The, 82–83
    High Priestess, The, 76–77
    Judgement, 112–113
    Justice, 94–95
    Lovers, The, 84–85
    Magician, The, 74–75
    Moon, The, 108–109
    Star, The, 106–107
    Strength, 88–89
    Sun, The, 110–111
    Temperance, 100–101
    Tower, The, 104–105
    Wheel of Fortune, 19, 92–93
    World, The, 114–115

Meditation, 62–68
Minor Arcana, 3, 22–23
   card meanings, 182–185
   Ace of Cups, 117, 118
   Ace of Pentacles, 133, 134
   Ace of Swords, 149, 150
   Ace of Wands, 163, 164
   Two of Cups, 117–119
   Two of Pentacles, 133–135
   Two of Swords, 149–151
   Two of Wands, 163–165
   Three of Cups, 118, 119–120
   Three of Pentacles, 134, 135
   Three of Swords, 150, 151
   Three of Wands, 164, 165–166
   Four of Cups, 120, 123
   Four of Pentacles, 136, 139
   Four of Swords, 150, 151–152
   Four of Wands, 166, 169
   Five of Cups, 120–121, 123
   Five of Pentacles, 136–137, 139
   Five of Swords, 150, 152–153
   Five of Wands, 167, 169
   Six of Cups, 121–122, 123
   Six of Pentacles, 137–138, 139
   Six of Swords, 153, 156
   Six of Wands, 168, 169
   Seven of Cups, 122–124
   Seven of Pentacles, 138–139
   Seven of Swords, 154, 156
   Seven of Wands, 168–170
   Eight of Cups, 124, 126
   Eight of Pentacles, 140, 142
   Eight of Swords, 154–155, 156
   Eight of Wands, 170–171, 172
   Nine of Cups, 124–125, 126
   Nine of Pentacles, 140–141, 142
   Nine of Swords, 155–156
   Nine of Wands, 171–173
   Ten of Cups, 125–127
   Ten of Pentacles, 141–143
   Ten of Swords, 156–157
   Ten of Wands, 172–173
   Page of Cups, 127–128, 130
   Page of Pentacles, 143–144, 145
   Page of Swords, 157–158, 160
   Page of Wands, 174, 176
   Knight of Cups, 128–129, 130
   Knight of Pentacles, 144–146
   Knight of Swords, 158–159, 160
   Knight of Wands, 174–175, 176
   Queen of Cups, 129–131
   Queen of Pentacles, 145, 146
   Queen of Swords, 159–160
   Queen of Wands, 175–177
   King of Cups, 130, 131
   King of Pentacles, 145, 147
   King of Swords, 160–161
   King of Wands, 176, 177
Moon, The, 108–109

N

Nine of Cups, 124–125, 126
Nine of Pentacles, 140–141, 142
Nine of Swords, 155–156
Nine of Wands, 171–173
Numbers, 22–23
   0 (The Fool), 72–73
   I (The Magician), 74–75
   II (The High Priestess), 76–77
   III (The Empress), 78–79
   IV (The Emperor), 80–81
   V (The Hierophant), 82–83
   VI (The Lovers), 84–85
   VII (The Chariot), 86–87
   VIII (Strength), 88–89

Numbers (*continued*)
  IX (The Hermit), 90–91
  X (Wheel of Fortune), 19, 92–93
  XI (Justice), 94–95
  XII (The Hanged Man), 96–97
  XIII (Death), 98–99
  XIV (Temperance), 100–101
  XV (The Devil), 102–103
  XVI (The Tower), 104–105
  XVII (The Star), 106–107
  XVIII (The Moon), 108–109
  XIX (The Sun), 110–111
  XX (Judgement), 112–113
  XXI (The World), 114–115
Numerology, 19

O

One-card meditation, 64–65
One-Card Pull, 29, 32–33

P

Page of Cups, 127–128, 130
Page of Pentacles, 143–144, 145
Page of Swords, 157–158, 160
Page of Wands, 174, 176
Pages, 23
Past/Present/Future spread, 36–37
Pentacles, 22, 132
  card meanings, 183
  Ace of Pentacles, 133, 134
  Two of Pentacles, 133–135
  Three of Pentacles, 134, 135
  Four of Pentacles, 136, 139
  Five of Pentacles, 136–137, 139
  Six of Pentacles, 137–138, 139
  Seven of Pentacles, 138–139
  Eight of Pentacles, 140, 142
  Nine of Pentacles, 140–141, 142
  Ten of Pentacles, 141–143
  Page of Pentacles, 143–144, 145
  Knight of Pentacles, 144–146
  Queen of Pentacles, 145, 146
  King of Pentacles, 145, 147
Positive qualities, 68

Q

Queen of Cups, 129–131
Queen of Pentacles, 145, 146
Queen of Swords, 159–160
Queen of Wands, 175–177
Queens, 23

R

Readings. *See also* Spreads
  beginner's, 26, 27
  preparing for, 13
  reading the cards, 17
  shuffling the deck, 16–17
  spiritual associations, 18–19
  spreads, 24–25
  stating your question, 13, 16
Relationship spread, 50–53
Reversals, 24–25
Rider-Waite-Smith deck, 4, 5, 6, 11
Rosicrucianism, 19

S

Self-discovery, 9, 62–68
Septenaries, 20
Seven of Cups, 122–124
Seven of Pentacles, 138–139
Seven of Swords, 154, 156
Seven of Wands, 168–170
Sforza, Francesco, 3
Signifier cards, 30–31
Six of Cups, 121–122, 123

Six of Pentacles, 137–138, 139
Six of Swords, 153, 156
Six of Wands, 168, 169
Smith, Pamela Colman, 4, 5–6
Spiritual traditions, 7, 9
Spreads, 24–25
    Celtic Cross, 45–49
    Comparing Your Options, 54–57
    Essential Keys, 42–44
    Let Go/Grow, 34–35
    Life Path, 38–41
    mediation on, 65
    One-Card Pull, 29, 32–33
    Past/Present/Future, 36–37
    Relationship, 50–53
    significator, 30–31
    Triquetra Outcome Management, 58–60
Star, The, 106–107
Stieglitz, Alfred, 5
Strength, 88–89
Sun, The, 110–111
Swords, 22, 148
    card meanings, 184
    Ace of Swords, 149, 150
    Two of Swords, 149–151
    Three of Swords, 150, 151
    Four of Swords, 150, 151–152
    Five of Swords, 150, 152–153
    Six of Swords, 153, 156
    Seven of Swords, 154, 156
    Eight of Swords, 154–155, 156
    Nine of Swords, 155–156
    Ten of Swords, 156–157
    Page of Swords, 157–158, 160
    Knight of Swords, 158–159, 160
    Queen of Swords, 159–160
    King of Swords, 160–161
Symbolism, 9, 14–15

Chariot, The, 87
Death, 99
Devil, The, 103
Emperor, The, 81
Empress, The, 79
Fool, The, 73
Hanged Man, The, 97
Hermit, The, 91
Hierophant, The, 83
High Priestess, The, 77
Judgement, 113
Justice, 95
Lovers, The, 85
Magician, The, 75
Moon, The, 109
Star, The, 107
Strength, 89
Sun, The, 111
Temperance, 101
Tower, The, 105
Wheel of Fortune, 92–93
World, The, 114–115

T

Tarot. *See also* Decks; Readings
    best practices for beginners, 8
    growing from, 62–68
    origins of, 3–4
    spiritual traditions in, 7, 9
    symbolism in, 9, 14–15
    using, 4, 6
Temperance, 100–101
Ten of Cups, 125–127
Ten of Pentacles, 141–143
Ten of Swords, 156–157
Ten of Wands, 172–173
Three of Cups, 118, 119–120
Three of Pentacles, 134, 135

Three of Swords, 150, 151
Three of Wands, 164, 165–166
Tower, The, 104–105
Tree of Life, 18
Triquetra Outcome Management spread, 58–60
Two of Cups, 117–119
Two of Pentacles, 133–135
Two of Swords, 149–151
Two of Wands, 163–165

U

Upright meanings, 24–25

V

Visconti, Bianca Maria, 3
Visconti, Filippo Maria, 3
Visconti-Sforza deck, 3–4, 19

W

Waite, A. E., 4, 18
Wands, 22, 162

card meanings, 184
Ace of Wands, 163, 164
Two of Wands, 163–165
Three of Wands, 164, 165–166
Four of Wands, 166, 169
Five of Wands, 167, 169
Six of Wands, 168, 169
Seven of Wands, 168–170
Eight of Wands, 170–171, 172
Nine of Wands, 171–173
Ten of Wands, 172–173
Page of Wands, 174, 176
Knight of Wands, 174–175, 176
Queen of Wands, 175–177
King of Wands, 176, 177
Wheel of Fortune, 19, 92–93
World, The, 114–115

Z

Zodiac signs, 15, 18

ACKNOWLEDGMENTS

I would like to thank my parents for believing in me. My endless gratitude goes to all of my creative writing teachers throughout the years who unwittingly taught me to read the tarot. Especially Regina Louise, Carolyn Cooke, and Gina Franco. Thank you to my tarot friends Susannah White and Alia Curtis. Written in loving memory of Tasha. Nana Twumasi, thank you for your wonderful editing and for being the mastermind behind this book. Leigh Saffold and Elizabeth Castoria, thank you for this opportunity. Thank you, Carol Rosenberg, and everyone at Callisto, for making this book happen. Harriet and Rohan: we knew each other when. Finally, thank you to Alan Clark, my partner in love and ontological crime, for his endless inspiration, hilarity and support.

ABOUT THE AUTHOR

MEG HAYERTZ is the founder of Creative Momentum, where she uses the tarot to help writers, artists, performers, and academics unlock creative blocks, deepen their inspiration, and finish their projects. She holds an MFA in writing and consciousness from California Institute of Integral Studies, and believes that creating is an act of listening. Also, she believes in you.

VISIT HER AT CreativeMomentum.art

CPSIA information can be obtained
at www.ICGtesting.com
Printed in the USA
JSHW010007190520
5746JS00002B/6

9 781623 159658